TREASURY OF AMERICAN DRAWINGS

TREASURY OF

American Drawings

CHARLES E. SLATKIN and REGINA SHOOLMAN

NEW YORK
OXFORD UNIVERSITY PRESS
1947

TO THE MEMORY OF

'SPUNKY'
(s.s.)

AMONG THE EARLIEST CASUALTIES

IN THE SECOND WORLD CONFLICT

Authors' Preface

As APPLIED TO the selections reproduced in the present volume, the term 'drawing' retains its broadest meaning, embracing not only the *pensée*, the tentatively launched idea, but the study sheet and the finished sketch as well. It includes the water-colored and gouache drawing, as extension of wash in the direction of tone (not always readily distinguishable from gouache or water-color painting), and the preparatory drawing executed in oil with brush (as was the custom with Gilbert Stuart, who did almost no other drawing), where it represents the preliminary attempt to define the subject, shaping it out of the blank area into protoplastic reality. The oil or water-colored sketch may thus more nearly approximate the groping of the artist's mind and hand in search of expressive form and contour than the highly finished study in pencil or charcoal. On the other hand, the full range of the draughtsman's peculiar media—the pen, pencil, charcoal, and crayon—is exemplified, while the pastel, whose full use comes too close to that of the finished oil painting, is generally excluded.

Drawing thus conceived, the editors' selection was not limited by any medium, though the intrusion of color promptly limited the degree of finish that the drawing might possess while still retaining the generic designation. In short, the present compilation excludes pastels and water colors as such and, thus delimited, seeks, where it can find examples in public collections, to demonstrate the peculiar syntax of form and linear design that characterizes the work of American artists.

That no serious effort has heretofore been made to exhibit such a group of originals [1] is evidence of the fact that American drawings have been too long neglected by our museums as well as by patrons beguiled by the glamor of the color sym-

[1] The Albany Institute of Arts and Sciences is perhaps a notable exception.

phony to the exclusion of the sonata, by the operatic glitter to the neglect of the chamber fugue.

Perhaps more truly than in any other country, America's artists reflect her folkways, her social and political ideals, her development as a nation and an idea. Of the individual qualities of the men who recorded her traits, of their temper and aesthetic timbre, the private sketch 'diaries' afford us our most intimate glance. Their major problem was to find their way against successive waves of influence from foreign shores, to find the means of expressing themselves and of speaking for their countrymen. To do this in the one nation in the world built solely out of an idea rather than a national stock, meant the inevitable development of a graphic equivalent in style, theme, and iconographic invention.

By analogy, the literary arts have shocked or stimulated us to self-discovery and interpretation through the folklore of a Bunyan, the Yankee head on Greek shoulders of an Emerson, the solitary grandeur of a Thoreau, the Hebraic voice of a Melville, the scriptural and liturgical outpouring of a Whitman. These are America, its speech patterns, its idioms, its ways of thinking. In Copley, in Ryder and Homer and Eakins and Bellows, and in scores of others, we have their visual equivalent. Inklings of our native genius in graphic terms, the primary evidence of our perceptual idioms and patterns, our ways of seeing, are to be found in the following pages.[2]

[2] The proper investigation of American art should lead, as one critic puts it, to 'a discovery of what, in all the production of that art, has flowered into a picturing of our own experience and mentality. . . Becoming aware of it is one way of making a home for ourselves in the universe and in that act becoming a mature and coherent people.' Virgil Barker, *A Critical Introduction to American Painting*, New York, 1931, pp. 39-40.

One is struck with the realization, in comparing American draughtsmanship with that of the great European tradition, that it is often fumbling and uncertain, closer to student effort than to that of the masters. The thinking, too, is sometimes fuzzy, the feeling and insight less than profound, the visual dialect limited, its syntax resting largely on verbs with few of the subtle participles and gerundives. And yet, here and there, like flashes of pure intuition, appears a drawing which, while it is indisputably native and local, as it should be, represents an astonishing seizure of the theme in its essence, is rendered lyrically with extraordinary freshness and vigor and invested with a significance that marks it as art of a first-rate order. Wherever possible, such qualities were borne in mind when the present samplings were made.

Within its own special field the present volume is merely introductory and represents a preliminary task of assemblage where none has hitherto been undertaken. It is the first of a four-volume survey of drawings that is intended to place the best of what lies in the public domain within easy reach of that same public.

Acknowledgments

WITHOUT the aid of many individuals in several score museums, libraries, and historical societies who have given generously of time and advice, much of the material in the present volume could not have been assembled. To the directors and assistants of the organizations represented in the following pages, the authors tender their warmest thanks. With certain of these, more direct contact and assistance have placed the authors in special debt. Particular thanks, therefore, are herewith expressed to Mr. John Davis Hatch, Jr., Director of the Albany Institute of Arts and Sciences, whose own work in this field has been most extensive and who generously made some of the materials in his files available; to Professor Frank Jewett Mather, Jr., of Princeton University, who was most helpful with suggestions and materials; to Drs. Hans Tietze and E. Conrat-Tietze, who assisted in some final deletions of illustrations; to Miss Agnes Mongan of the Fogg Museum of Art, and Dr. Heinrich Schwarz of the Rhode Island School of Design Museum, as well as their respective assistants, Miss Helen D. Willard and Miss Florence Mellowes. Miss Alice M. Sharkey at the Whitney Museum and Miss Una E. Johnson, Curator of Prints and Drawings at the Brooklyn Museum, facilitated the securing of photographs of unpublished materials, while Mr. Harry B. Wehle, Curator of Paintings at the Metropolitan Museum of Art, and Mr. Alan Burroughs offered helpful critical suggestions on portions of the text which they read. Mr. R. N. Williams, 2nd, Director of the Historical Society of Pennsylvania, and Mr. John H. Powell, Assistant-Librarian of the Free Library of Philadelphia, provided access to important photographic and documentary material. Mr. R. W. G. Vail, Director of the New-York Historical Society, enabled the authors to study and reproduce several little-known drawings by Boardman Robinson, while Miss Dorothy C. Barck, Librarian, and Mr. Arthur B. Carlson, Assistant at the Society, facilitated the task of research and the gathering of photographs. Miss Grace M. Mayer of the Museum of the City of New York; Miss Muriel C. Figenbaum of the Boston Public Library; Mr. H. Rossiter and Mr. Austin Mitchell of the Boston Museum of Fine Arts; Miss Elmira Bier of the Phillips Memorial Gallery in Washington; Mr. Philip C. Beam at Bowdoin College; Mr. Bartlett H. Hayes, Director, and Miss Mary C. Rathbun, Research Assistant, at the Addison Gallery, Andover, Mass.; Mr. James Thrall Soby, former Curator, and his Assistant, Miss Mimi Catlin, at the Museum of Modern Art; Mr. Theodore Bolton of the Century Association; Dr. Rudolf Berliner, formerly at Cooper Union Museum; Mr. Dwight Kirsch at the University of Nebraska; Mr. Henry Sayles Francis, Curator, Cleveland Museum; and Mr. Karl Küp, Curator of Prints at the New York Public Library, all have been generous with suggestions and data on the drawings in their collections. The authors were also greatly aided in their search for unpublished material by the Babcock, Albert Duveen, Bland, Downtown, Knoedler, Kraushaar, Macbeth, and Rehn Galleries. A number of artists, notably John Sloan, Everett Shinn, and Stuart Davis offered, in discussion, information of interest, which helped to establish the background of art schools and movements. A number of other individuals were generously helpful, and the omission of their names—a concession to the proprieties of space—only increases the authors' indebtedness. Yet here especially, room must be allowed for homage to an extraordinary eye, that of Dr. Léo Bronstein.

C. E. S.
R. S.

New York, January 1946

List of Illustrations

Plates arranged alphabetically according to artist. Plate numbers are given in parentheses; measurements in inches.

CALDER, ALEXANDER 1898-1945
Lion Tamer (148)
Pen; 12½ x 14
Collection: Philadelphia Museum of Art, Philadelphia, Pa.

CARROLL, JOHN 1892-
Head (120)
Pencil; 19⅜ x 12¹⁄₁₆
Collection: Brooklyn Museum, Brooklyn, N. Y.

CASSATT, MARY 1845-1926
Girl Seated (94)
Pencil; 8¹¹⁄₁₆ x 6³⁄₁₆
Collection: Cleveland Museum of Art, Cleveland, Ohio

CATLIN, GEORGE 1796-1872
War Dance (39)
India ink; 10½ x 25¼
Collection: U. S. National Museum, Smithsonian Institution, Washington, D. C.

CHASE, WILLIAM MERRITT 1849-1916
Seated Woman (92)
India ink wash, black crayon on cardboard; 17 x 13¾
Collection: Cooper Union Museum, New York City

CHURCH, FREDERICK E. 1826-1900
The Heart of the Andes (41)
Pencil; 8 x 13⁷⁄₁₆
Collection: City Art Museum, St. Louis, Mo.
Seascape (43)
Pencil; 6½ x 6½ in circ. mat
Collection: Albany Institute of History and Art, Albany, N. Y.

COLE, THOMAS 1801-1848
Landscape (42)
Pencil; 3¾ x 5⅛
Collection: New-York Historical Society, New York City
Landscape with Tower (46)
Pencil; 8½ x 6½
Collection: Metropolitan Museum of Art, New York City

COLEMAN, GLENN O. 1887-1932
Street Bathers (104)
Lithograph crayon; 11¼ x 15⅞
Collection: Whitney Museum of American Art, New York City

COLMAN, SAMUEL 1832-1920
Wind-Blown Pines, Pacific Grove, California (83)
Pencil, white gouache, brown water-color wash on brown paper; 10¾ x 14½
Collection: Cooper Union Museum, New York City

COPLEY, JOHN SINGLETON 1732-1815
Troop Maneuvers (2)
Sepia ink; 3⅜ x 7
Collection: Addison Gallery of American Art, Phillips Academy, Andover, Mass.
Mrs. Ebenezer Storer (3)
Pastel on paper; 24 x 18
Metropolitan Museum of Art, New York City
Head of the Earl of Bathurst, Lord Chancellor (drawing for the *Death of the Earl of Chatham*) (5)
Black and white chalk on gray-blue paper; 26 x 19½
Collection: Museum of Fine Arts (M. and M. Karolik Collection), Boston, Mass.
Study for the Central Figure of *Monmouth before James II* (6)
Pencil heightened with white on blue paper; 13¾ x 11¼
Collection: Fogg Museum of Art, Harvard University, Cambridge, Mass.
Study for *Brooke Watson and the Shark* (7)
Pen and wash; 19⅛ x 23½
Collection: Museum of Historic Art, Princeton University, Princeton, N. J.
Studies of Central Group and of Fleeing Woman and Child for *The Death of Major Pierson* (8)
Pencil, crayon, and white chalk on gray-blue paper; 13¾ x 22¼
Collection: Museum of Fine Arts (M. and M. Karolik Collection), Boston, Mass.

CORBINO, JON 1905-
Conflict (144)
Charcoal; 21 x 29
Collection: Kleeman Gallery, New York City
Laughing Angel (157)
Tempera and oil drawing; 34¼ x 23¼
Collection: Whitney Museum of American Art, New York City

CURRY, JOHN STEUART 1897-1946
Head of a Negro (142)
Brown chalk; 20⅝ x 15⅝
Collection: Whitney Museum of American Art, New York City

DARLEY, FELIX O. C. 1822-1888
Conestoga Wagon (52)
Wash; 10 x 14
Collection: Historical Society of Pennsylvania, Philadelphia, Pa.

DAVIS, STUART 1894-
Flower Study–Compote (133)
Brush; 24½ x 18½
Collection: Whitney Museum of American Art, New York City

DEHN, ADOLF 1895-
Lake and Trees (159)
Ink and wash; 12½ x 19
Collection: Addison Gallery of American Art, Phillips Academy, Andover, Mass.
Sunday Stroll (149)

Ink and wash; 12½ x 19
Collection: The Museum of Modern Art (Gift of Mrs. John D. Rockefeller, Jr.), New York City

DEWING, THOMAS WILMER 1851-1938
Head of a Girl (90)
Silverpoint; 16¼ x 13¾
Collection: National Collection of Fine Arts, Smithsonian Institution (Gift of John Gellatly), Washington, D. C.

DICKINSON, PRESTON 1891-1930
Self Portrait (132)
Charcoal on gray-white paper; 17⅞ x 11⁹⁄₁₆
Collection: Fogg Museum of Art, Harvard University (Paul J. Sachs Collection), Cambridge, Mass.

DOUGHTY, THOMAS 1793-1856
River Scene (33)
Pencil; 5¹⁵⁄₁₆ x 7½
Collection: Metropolitan Museum of Art, New York City

DU BOIS, GUY PÈNE 1884-
Conversation (113)
Pen and colored wash; 9⅝ x 10
Collection: Whitney Museum of American Art, New York City

DURAND, ASHER B. 1796-1886
Landscape (40)
Wash drawing on tan paper; 9⅛ x 12¾
Collection: Addison Gallery of American Art, Phillips Academy, Andover, Mass.
Rural Scene (44)
Pencil; 8⅛ x 7
Collection: New-York Historical Society, New York City
Sketch from Nature (45)
Pencil on gray paper; 14 x 10
Collection: Metropolitan Museum of Art, New York City

DUVENECK, FRANK 1848-1919
Double Self Portrait (89)
Pen and ink; 11¼ x 7⅞
Collection: Cincinnati Art Museum, Cincinnati, Ohio
Head of a Young Girl (91)
Black chalk; 9¼ x 7¼
Collection: Cincinnati Art Museum, Cincinnati, Ohio

EAKINS, THOMAS 1844-1916
Masked Woman Seated (81)
Charcoal; 24 x 18
Collection: Philadelphia Museum of Art, Philadelphia, Pa.
Study for The Gross Clinic (80)
Pen drawing; 11¾ x 14¾
Collection: Philadelphia Museum of Art, Philadelphia, Pa.
Perspective Drawing and Study of John Biglen (87)
Pencil, pen, and colored washes; 28 x 46
Collection: Whitney Museum of American Art, New York City

Negro Boy Dancing (88)
Water-colored drawing; 18½ x 22⅝
Collection: Metropolitan Museum of Art, New York City

FLANNAGAN, JOHN B. 1895-1942
Whippet (141)
Crayon; 10 x 13⅞
Collection: Seattle Art Museum (Fuller Collection), Seattle, Washington

GLACKENS, WILLIAM JAMES 1870-1938
The Apple Seller (108)
Pencil; 9¾ x 8
Collection: Kraushaar Art Galleries, New York City
Washington Square, 1914 (106)
Pencil and wash; 24⅜ x 18
Collection: Museum of Modern Art (Gift of Mrs. John D. Rockefeller, Jr.), New York City

GROPPER, WILLIAM 1897-
Farmers' Revolt (161)
Brush; 16¾ x 19½
Collection: Whitney Museum of American Art, New York City

GROSS, CHAIM 1904-
Acrobats (152)
Ink and wash; 13⅝ x 12¾
Collection: Addison Gallery of American Art, Phillips Academy, Andover, Mass.

GROSZ, GEORGE 1893-
Portrait Study (145)
Pencil; 27 x 21
Collection: Museum of Modern Art (Gift of Paul J. Sachs), New York City

GROTH, JOHN 1908-
Air Raid (162)
Ink; 15 x 18½
Collection: Brooklyn Museum, Brooklyn, N. Y.

HART, GEORGE OVERBURY ('POP') 1868-1933
The Jury (116)
Wash, charcoal and ink; 14¼ x 19¼
Collection: Museum of Modern Art (Gift of Mrs. John D. Rockefeller, Jr.), New York City

HARTLEY, MARSDEN 1877-1943
Landscape: Mount Katahdin (122)
Crayon; 21¼ x 26½
Collection: Fogg Museum of Art, Harvard University (Paul J. Sachs Collection), Cambridge, Mass.

HASSAM, CHILDE 1859-1935
Little Church around the Corner (95)
Pencil and chalk on cream paper; 7⅞ x 11⁹⁄₁₆
Collection: Fogg Museum of Art, Harvard University (Grenville L. Winthrop Collection), Cambridge, Mass.

HENRI, ROBERT 1865-1929
The Boatman (107)
Charcoal; 11 x 7½
Collection: Metropolitan Museum of Art, New York City

HENRY, EDWARD LAMSON 1841-1919
A New England Regiment Taking the Cars from Jersey City for the Front, April, 1864 (102)
Charcoal and white chalk; 12¼ x 19¾
Collection: Museum of Historic Art, Princeton University, Princeton, N. J.

HIGGINS, EUGENE 1874-
Adrift (117)
Water color on paper; 15¼ x 20¾
Collection: Metropolitan Museum of Art, New York City

HILL, JOHN W. 1770-1850
Broadway and Trinity Church, 1830 (27)
Water-colored drawing; 13⅝ x 9⅝
Collection: New York Public Library, New York City

HOMER, WINSLOW 1836-1910
The Unruly Calf (62)
Pencil heightened with white on gray paper; 4⅝ x 8¾
Collection: Brooklyn Museum, Brooklyn, N. Y.
The Last Boat In (75)
Crayon; 8¼ x 12
Collection: Addison Gallery of American Art, Phillips Academy, Andover, Mass.
Boy Picking Berries (77)
Pencil heightened with white on tan paper; 4⅝ x 4¼
Collection: Addison Gallery of American Art, Phillips Academy, Andover, Mass.
Banks Fishermen (78)
Black and white crayon on blue-gray paper; 16⅝ x 20⅝
Collection: Cooper Union Museum, New York City
Flamboro Head, England (79)
Drawing with gouache and wash; 17½ x 23½
Collection: Art Institute of Chicago (Mr. and Mrs. M. A. Ryerson Collection), Chicago, Ill.
Study of a Soldier (76)
Black chalk, heightened in white; 13¼ x 8¼
Collection: Cincinnati Art Museum, Cincinnati, Ohio

HOPPER, EDWARD 1882-
Study for *Manhattan Bridge Loop* (118)
Charcoal; 8½ x 11
Collection: Addison Gallery of American Art, Phillips Academy, Andover, Mass.

HUNT, WILLIAM MORRIS 1824-1879
Sketch for *The Bathers* (59)
Charcoal; 19 x 15⅝
Collection: Worcester Art Museum (Gift of Robert Woods Bliss), Worcester, Mass.
Portrait Study (60)
Charcoal; 10¼ x 10

Collection: Museum of Historic Art, Princeton University, Princeton, N. J.

INMAN, HENRY 1801-1845
Portrait of a Man (29)
Crayon; 13¼ x 10
Collection: Addison Gallery of American Art, Phillips Academy, Andover, Mass.
Illustration for *The Betrothed* (35)
Sepia wash; 3½ x 5
Collection: New-York Historical Society, New York City
Red Jacket (37)
Pencil; 6⅞ x 5⅛
Collection: Albany Institute of History and Art (Gift of Sarah DeWitt), Albany, N. Y.

INNESS, GEORGE 1825-1894
Woodland Bank (66)
Crayon on cream-gray paper; 10¼ x 14½
Collection: Fogg Museum of Art, Harvard University, Cambridge, Mass.
Landscape (67)
Pencil on tinted paper; 9 x 5¾
Collection: The Free Library, Philadelphia, Pa.

JOHNSON, EASTMAN 1824-1906
Polly Gary (61)
Charcoal and chalk; 18½ x 14
Collection: Addison Gallery of American Art, Phillips Academy, Andover, Mass.
Study for *The Boy Lincoln* (86)
Charcoal heightened with white on brown paper; 15½ x 13½
Collection: Robert Fridenberg Gallery, New York City
Berry Pickers (63)
Pencil and water color on brown paper; 7¾ x 19⅜
Collection: Addison Gallery of American Art, Phillips Academy, Andover, Mass.
Secretary Dobbins (64)
Charcoal heightened with white on brown paper; 26⅞ x 19
Collection: Addison Gallery of American Art, Phillips Academy, Andover, Mass.
Miss Ward (65)
Charcoal on gray-tan paper; 19¾ x 15
Collection: Addison Gallery of American Art, Phillips Academy, Andover, Mass.

JOHNSTON, DAVID CLAYPOOLE 1797-1865
Ginger Beer Stall (51)
Water-colored drawing; 9¼ x 12⅜
Collection: American Antiquarian Society, Worcester, Mass.

KANTOR, MORRIS 1896-
Study of a Head (134)
Red chalk; 24 x 17¾
Collection: Brooklyn Museum, Brooklyn, N. Y.

KUHN, WALT 1880-
Woman Clown (119)

Ink; 16 x 11½
Collection: University of Arizona, Gallery of Modern
American Paintings, Tucson, Arizona

KUNIYOSHI, YASUO 1893-
Skaters (150)
Charcoal and pen and ink; 12⅜ x 16¾
Collection: Addison Gallery of American Art, Phillips
Academy, Andover, Mass.

LACHAISE, GASTON 1882-1935
Nude Study (154)
Pencil; 18 x 12
Collection: Whitney Museum of American Art, New York
City

LA FARGE, JOHN 1835-1910
Figure Studies (72)
Charcoal on gray canvas; 38 x 25
Collection: Whitney Museum of American Art, New York
City
The Three Marys (73)
Pencil; 12½ x 10¼
Collection: Museum of Historic Art, Princeton University,
Princeton, N. J.

LEBRUN, RICO 1900-
Reclining Ox (140)
Charcoal; 9 x 12
Collection: Fogg Museum of Art, Harvard University
(Anonymous Loan), Cambridge, Mass.

LEUTZE, EMANUEL 1816-1868
Head of a Woman (57)
Pencil, crayon, and water color; 3⅞ x 5⅜
Collection: Addison Gallery of American Art, Phillips
Academy, Andover, Mass.
Study of Hands (57)
Pencil, crayon, and water color; 4 x 5¾
Collection: Addison Gallery of American Art, Phillips
Academy, Andover, Mass.

LUKS, GEORGE 1867-1933
Studies of Men's Heads (105)
Charcoal; 8 x 10⅝
Collection: Museum of Historic Art, Princeton University,
Princeton, N. J.
L. Waterbury at Polo (109)
Black crayon; 9⅜ x 6⅝
Collection: Metropolitan Museum of Art, New York City

McFEE, HENRY LEE 1886-
The City (127)
Pencil; 20 x 14¼
Collection: Addison Gallery of American Art, Phillips
Academy, Andover, Mass.
Hands (128)
Pencil; 12 x 13
Collection: Bowdoin College Museum, Brunswick, Me.

MALBONE, EDWARD G. 1777-1807
Self Portrait (23)
Oil and sepia wash; 29 x 24½
Collection: Providence Athenaeum, Providence, R. I.

MARSH, REGINALD 1898-
Girl Walking (135)
Wash; 20 x 14
Collection: Whitney Museum of American Art, New York
City

MARTIN, HOMER DODGE 1836-1897
Street Scene (71)
Wash drawing on white paper; 10 x 9
Collection: Addison Gallery of American Art, Phillips
Academy, Andover, Mass.
Sketch in the Adirondacks (74)
Pencil; 12½ x 20¹¹⁄₁₆
Collection: City Art Museum, St. Louis, Mo.

MORAN, THOMAS 1837-1926
Spanish Peak, Colorado (82)
Pencil, gray water-color wash; 7¾ x 5¹⁄₁₆
Collection: Cooper Union Museum, New York City

MORSE, SAMUEL F. B. 1791-1872
*Mrs. Richard C. Morse and Two Children, Elizabeth
and Charlotte* (21)
Pencil with touches of white chalk; 17 x 11⅞
Collection: Macbeth Gallery (Collection of Russell Col-
gate, West Orange, N. J.), New York City
Romantic Scene (34)
Pencil; 2⅞ x 4¾
Collection: New-York Historical Society, New York City

MOUNT, WILLIAM SIDNEY 1807-1868
Portrait of a Lady (55)
Pencil; 9¾ x 7¹¹⁄₁₆
Collection: Fogg Museum of Art, Harvard University,
Cambridge, Mass.
Sketches (56)
Pencil; 12¼ x 7⅞
Collection: Addison Gallery of American Art, Phillips
Academy, Andover, Mass.
Midshipman Seabury (58)
Pencil; 9⅞ x 7⅝
Collection: Suffolk Museum (Melville Collection), Stony
Brook, Long Island

NAST, THOMAS 1840-1902
Tammany Tiger (84)
Crayon; 14½ x 21½
Collection: Addison Gallery of American Art, Phillips
Academy, Andover, Mass.

NEAGLE, JOHN 1796-1865
Francis Grice (22)
Pencil on brown paper; 8¼ x 10½
Collection: The Free Library, Philadelphia, Pa.

NEAGLE, JOHN 1796-1865 (Continued)
Sketches (36)
Pencil; 7¾ x 11
Collection: Addison Gallery of American Art, Phillips Academy, Andover, Mass.

O'KEEFE, GEORGIA 1887-
Eagle Claw and Bean Necklace (123)
Charcoal; 18⅞ x 25⅛
Collection: Museum of Modern Art (Anonymous Gift), New York City

PASCIN, JULES 1885-1930
Self Portrait (147)
Transfer paper drawing; 19 x 12
Collection: Museum of Modern Art (Gift of Mrs. John D. Rockefeller, Jr.), New York City

PEALE, CHARLES WILLSON 1741-1827
Ferry Three Miles below Bristol (15)
Pencil; 15⅛ x 8½
Collection: The Free Library, Philadelphia, Pa.

PEALE, REMBRANDT 1778-1860
Harpers Ferry in 1812 (20)
Water-color sketch; 10 x 13
Collection: Municipal Museum of the City of Baltimore, Baltimore, Md.
Portrait Sketch of Robert Owen (31)
Pencil heightened with white chalk; 15½ x 11⅝
Collection: Albert Duveen Gallery, New York City

PRENDERGAST, MAURICE 1861-1924
On the Shore (103)
Water color and pastel; 17½ x 22
Collection: Kraushaar Art Galleries, New York City

ROBINSON, BOARDMAN 1876-
Frontier Guard, Macedonia (126)
Charcoal, pen, and wash; 13½ x 10¾
Collection: New-York Historical Society, New York City
The Master of the House (125)
Ink; 9 x 5
Collection: New-York Historical Society, New York City
It Was the Wrong Time to Say the Right Thing (131)
Brush and ink; 21⅛ x 16¹⁵⁄₁₆
Collection: Metropolitan Museum of Art, New York City
Draped Nude (156)
Pencil with colored washes; 14 x 10
Collection: Whitney Museum of American Art, New York City

ST. MEMIN, C. B. J., DE 1770-1852
An Indian Girl of the 'Iowas of the Missouri' (38)
Crayon on pink tinted paper; 23 x 17
Collection: New-York Historical Society, New York City

SARGENT, JOHN SINGER 1856-1925
Male Nude in Action (97)
Charcoal; 25 x 19
Collection: Wellesley College Art Museum, Wellesley, Mass.
Figure Study: Man Standing, Hands on Head (98)
Charcoal on gray paper; 24½ x 18¾
Collection: Metropolitan Museum of Art, New York City
Duchess of Marlborough (Consuelo Vanderbilt) (99)
Pencil; 11⅛ x 7⅞
Collection: Metropolitan Museum of Art, New York City

SHEELER, CHARLES 1883-
Feline Felicity (151)
Conte crayon; 22 x 18
Collection: Fogg Museum of Art, Harvard University, Cambridge, Mass.

SHINN, EVERETT 1876-
Old Chinatown Restaurant (115)
Ink and water color; 9 x 12
Collection: Collection of the artist

SHIRLAW, WALTER 1838-1909
Studies for *Violin Player* (96)
Pencil, white crayon on rough gray paper; 19⁹⁄₁₆ x 15
Collection: Cooper Union Museum, New York City

SIPORIN, MITCHELL 1910-
Engineers at Gaeta (155)
Ink; 13½ x 19
Collection: U. S. War Department, Washington, D. C.

SLOAN, JOHN 1871-
McSorley's Cats (110)
Black crayon on white paper; 17⅛ x 21⅛
Collection: Fogg Museum of Art, Harvard University (Paul J. Sachs Collection), Cambridge, Mass.
State Police in Philadelphia (111)
Crayon; 21 x 30
Collection: Collection of the artist

SMIBERT, JOHN 1688-1751
Cosimo III de Medici (4)
Black crayon heightened with white; 5¼ x 6½
Collection: Bowdoin College Museum, Brunswick, Me.

SOYER, RAPHAEL 1899-
Study of an Old Man (136)
Ink on cream paper; 9¾ x 5¾
Collection: Addison Gallery of American Art, Phillips Academy, Andover, Mass.

SPEICHER, EUGENE 1883-
Red Moore (143)
Charcoal; 12⅜ x 9¼
Collection: Addison Gallery of American Art, Phillips Academy, Andover, Mass.

STERNE, MAURICE 1877-
Balinese Girl (130)
Charcoal; 14½ x 18¾
Collection: San Francisco Museum of Art, San Francisco, Cal.

STUART, GILBERT 1755-1828
Self Portrait (14)
Ink
Collection: Location Unknown

SULLY, THOMAS 1783-1872
Sketch Sheet (28)
Ink and wash; 8½ x 11¼
Collection: Addison Gallery of American Art, Phillips Academy, Andover, Mass.
Woman and Child Reading (30)
Pencil and wash; 8⅛ x 7
Collection: New-York Historical Society, New York City
Man's Head (32)
Crayon; 8½ x 6½
Collection: Philadelphia Museum of Art, Philadelphia, Pa.

TAYLOR, CHARLES JAY 1855-1929
Madison Square, 1892 (100)
Water-colored drawing; 15⅝ x 6
Collection: Museum of the City of New York (J. Clarence Davies Collection), New York City

TRUMBULL, JOHN 1756-1843
Death of Hotspur (16)
Brown ink with sketches in pencil; 8¾ x 7
Collection: Vassar College Museum, Poughkeepsie, N. Y.
Reclining Nude (17)
Black crayon, white chalk on blue-gray paper; 14⅛ x 24⅛
Collection: Yale University Art Gallery, New Haven, Conn.
General Hugh Mercer (18)
Pencil; 4⁵⁄₁₆ x 3⅛
Collection: Metropolitan Museum of Art, New York City
Officers Crying (19)
Charcoal; 15⅞ x 19½
Collection: Addison Gallery of American Art, Phillips Academy, Andover, Mass.

TWACHTMAN, JOHN HENRY 1853-1902
Footbridge at Bridgeport (101)
Pastel; 11¾ x 19½
Collection: Washington County Museum of Fine Arts (Gift of Mrs. Singer), Hagerstown, Md.

VANDERLYN, JOHN 1775?-1852
Sarah Russell Church (24)
Crayon; 8⁷⁄₁₆ x 6⅜
Collection: Metropolitan Museum of Art, New York City

WALKOWITZ, ABRAHAM 1880-
Man of Iron (129)
Charcoal; 12½ x 7½
Collection: Newark Museum, Newark, N. J.

WEBER, MAX, 1881-
Head of a Woman (124)
Charcoal on cardboard; 16⅛ x 13
Collection: Museum of Modern Art (Gift of Mrs. John D. Rockefeller, Jr.), New York City

WEIR, JULIAN ALDEN 1852-1919
Girl at the Piano (93)
Pencil; 10 x 8
Collection: Carnegie Institute, Pittsburgh, Pa.

WEST, BENJAMIN 1738-1820
Head of an Old Man (9)
Pencil on paper; 8⅛ x 6⅛
Collection: Benjamin West Society, Swarthmore, Pa.
David James Dove (10)
Pencil; 6½ x 3⅞
Collection: Historical Society of Pennsylvania, Philadelphia, Pa.
Doctor Bragg (11)
Pencil on paper; 6⅜ x 4⅝
Collection: Benjamin West Society, Swarthmore, Pa.
Figure Composition (12)
Brown ink; 7 x 6
Collection: Benjamin West Society, Swarthmore, Pa.
The Three Sisters (13)
Brown ink, sepia, and cobalt blue; 14½ x 11
Collection: William Rockhill Nelson Gallery, Atkins Museum of Fine Arts, Kansas City, Mo.

WHISTLER, JAMES ABBOTT McNEILL 1834-1903
Nude with a Fan (68)
Charcoal on paper; 11¼ x 7⅛
Collection: Metropolitan Museum of Art, New York City
Sketch for the *Portrait of Carlyle* (69)
Brown ink on gray-white paper; 6⅜ x 5⅝
Collection: Fogg Museum of Art, Harvard University (Grenville L. Winthrop Collection), Cambridge, Mass.
Venetian Canal (70)
Pastel on gray paper; 11 x 5
Collection: The Frick Collection, New York City

WOOD, GRANT 1892-1944
Dinner for Threshers (138)
Pencil on brown paper; 17¾ x 26¾
Collection: Whitney Museum of American Art, New York

YOUNG, MAHONRI 1877-
Boxer (160)
Black chalk on gray-pink paper; 19⅞ x 12¹⁵⁄₁₆
Collection: Fogg Museum of Art, Harvard University (Grenville L. Winthrop Collection), Cambridge, Mass.
The Shovellers (112)
Brush and ink; 8½ x 11⅛
Collection: Addison Gallery of American Art, Phillips Academy, Andover, Mass.

ZORACH, WILLIAM 1887-
The Artist's Daughter (153)
Ink; 11 x 8½
Collection: Newark Museum, Newark, N. J.

TREASURY OF AMERICAN DRAWINGS

A Colonial Choice

THE scarcity of early American drawings and sketches, forever subject to the vicissitudes of the artists' changing fortunes and the itinerants' shifting residences, is attributable in part to their fragile nature. On the other hand, a considerable body of incunabula, early seventeenth-century cartographers' drawings like the *Novum Amsterodamum* (1650) (Plate 1) in the New-York Historical Society, and of prints, beginning with that earliest known copperplate cut in North America, the *Mapp of Rariton River*, engraved in 1683 from a plate or drawing by John Reid, have come down to us in excellent state of preservation.

These neighborhood prospects were often framed and hung as decoration in colonial parlors, so that their chances of survival were of course generally enhanced. But the same interest was hardly attached to painters' personal sketches at a time when even oil paintings endured a precarious existence. Moreover, such early drawings were scarce to begin with, since artists who took scant trouble to sign portraits done at five to fifty dollars were even less likely to undertake preliminary sketches or to preserve them once the finished product was delivered. Portrait heads were for the most part blocked in with the brush, sometimes in sepia, and the likeness seized or sought in color. For the rest, to the limners, Sunday painters, local artisans, or professional itinerants, exclusively devoted to color portraits, the practice of thinking in lines subjectively, experimentally, or preparatorily was hardly part of the day's work or evening's study. Thus the possibility that many colonial drawings have been lost or destroyed,[1] or are now reposing in scattered attic trunks, is remote.

In Europe the cult of collecting drawings, *pensées*, preliminary sketches, cartoons for tapestries, and frescoes or finished studies was long established, with such valuation as Vasari or Lely, for example, placed upon them as the key to the artist's personality, the diary of his aesthetic life, the clues to his evolution, as well as the evidence for attribution of finished paintings—or simply as precious and delightful in themselves. But in America only a series of fortunate accidents could account for the survival of occasional sketchbooks and sheets to which even the artist attached but slight importance.

In 1729 John Smibert, the first thoroughly trained artist to work in America, arrived from Edinburgh in the entourage of Dean Berkeley. The artist, 'a silent, modest man, who abhorred the finesse of some of his profession,' apparently anticipated Hogarth's plea for an art based on 'realities' and his outburst against the 'portrait manufacturers' and 'phiz-mongers.' At any rate, Berkeley, one of the first British worthies to come to America with a Utopian scheme for founding an educational settlement in the Bermudas, easily persuaded Smibert to join the venture as teacher

[1] The Boston Fire of 1872 destroyed a number of paintings and sketches. One would give much to see examples of drawings by Smibert, Feke, Badger, Blackburn, Earl, and others. None has come to light, if we exclude the Smibert *Cosimo III* as a mere copy and Blackburn's pastels as belonging more properly to the category of painting. Earl's slight sketch of George Washington appeared in the Hewlett sale, but is of small consequence. Alan Burroughs lists a number of drawings by John Greenwood, done after his brief period of activity in America. Theodore Bolton, *Early American Portrait Draughtsmen in Crayons*, New York, 1923, lists some interesting items in this medium.

and master of the arts. If Hogarth's notion of portraiture appealed to Smibert, the Bishop's famous verse, ending 'Westward the course of empire takes its way,' appeared as a logical challenge. America might well be the Promised Land for an artist whose tastes were unpretentious and honest.

Although the Bishop's pretty idea failed to materialize for lack of financial support, he founded a grammar school at Northport, later attended by Gilbert Stuart, while Smibert settled in Boston. The latter had 'spent a fortune in Italy' on paintings of Roman ruins, landscapes, romantic scenes; on engravings, 'the best mezzotints, Italian, French, Dutch, and English prints in frames and glasses'; on drawings, purchased or done by his own hand; and had purchased or made copies after Raphael (*Madonna dell' Impannata*); Titian (*Venus and Cupid*); and Van Dyck (*Cardinal Bentivoglio*); casts (*Venus de Medici, Homer's Head,* 'perhaps the *Laocoön*').

Thus a symbolic propriety may be read into the *Cosimo III, Grand Duke of Tuscany* (Plate 4) at Bowdoin College, which tradition and signature have long assigned to the hand of Smibert. An image of European oligarchy, the present drawing marks, as it were, the transition to a New-World civilization. The bleary eyes, the idiotic expression of this astonishing portrait study, which may, as Professor Oskar Hagen argues,[2] be a copy after Magnasco, who was in Florence with Smibert, tell their tale of the bigoted tyrant for whom both artists worked. It remains a prototypic cartoon of all that gave meaning and direction to the colonists' and Smibert's own new venture. The artist appears to have deliberately abandoned a good measure of certain success and profit in Europe for the limited but more congenial opportunities in the new land. (Doubtless the opportunity to do portraits like that of Samuel Sewall compensated Smibert in a measure for the fact that he died in very modest circumstances, as the inventory of his estate reveals.)

Some three months after his arrival Smibert was already exhibiting his collection. And when he set up his art store of canvases, paints, palette knives,

[2] *The Birth of the American Tradition in Art,* New York, 1940.

books on perspective, and art works, as well as his studio, 'an appropriate appartment lined with green cloth or baise,' these became the center of transplanted tradition and inspiration. The apartment in due course was visited or rented by Samuel Minot, Charles Willson Peale, Copley, who lived near by, Trumbull, and Allston, among others. Here was much to attract the younger artists, eager for a breath of the grand tradition. How much they could accept and imitate, and what repudiate, would in the end be a matter of both individual instinct and the pressure of prevailing tastes, but a good deal of the initial refining process was to be here accomplished.

The struggle for political self-expression in the Colonies was another aspect of the same process of refining conflicting loyalties. The colonists were no sooner established in numbers than the inevitability of ultimate dichotomy was apparent. But the specific elements, the forces of alienation, the direction of ideological lines that would culminate in political separation from the Old World, were not readily discernible.[3]

In such a society it falls to the artist 'to give form to the life and character and emotions of a people, so that men may see themselves objectified in these subtle images and come to a harmony with themselves.'[4]

For colonial painters, the struggle between the European example and the native impulse to sober, factual, and unadorned presentation was a choice

[3] Reference need hardly be made to the rich treatment given these antagonisms and protagonisms in Vernon Parrington's monumental *Main Currents in American Thought,* New York, 1927, 3 vols.

Governor John Winthrop's was by no means a minority voice when he declared: 'Democracy is amongst civill nations accounted the meanest and worst of all forms of government.' Or that of Governor Berkeley of Virginia when he wrote: 'But I thank God *there are no free Schools* nor *printing* and I hope we shall not have these hundred years, for *learning* has brought disobedience and heresy, and sects into the world, and *printing* has developed them, and libels against the best government. God keep us from both.'

[4] E. P. Richardson, *American Romantic Painting,* New York, 1940, p. 20. Constance Rourke points out that 'Our painting has never been fully considered in its native cultural relations and implications or basic intentions. . .' (*Roots of American Culture,* New York, 1942, p. 286.) Several such volumes are now in preparation.

[4]

between opposing methods and points of view. The crystallization of an American tradition could come but slowly and against waves of influence from foreign shores: that of Van Dyck and the Italian Baroque through Smibert's properties and early work; of Highmore and Hudson through the early work of Feke and Blackburn; of fashion-plate portraiture in the aristocratic South, always closer to England, through the work of Wollaston, Theus, and Benbridge; of Kneller in the work of the elder Vanderlyn; and finally the studio of West and the example of certain of his students. If the foreign influence grew and repeatedly drew young Americans to British and Continental shores, the native psychology nevertheless persisted and renewed itself in scattered New England cities and later in Dutch New York and Quaker Philadelphia and the ever-expanding frontier to the West. Within a single lifetime, the political revolution of 1776, the Jeffersonian revolution of 1790 to 1800, the economic independence marked by the War of 1812, and the Jacksonian revolution of 1832, came as successive crises of self-revelation, sustaining and reaffirming a common faith in the average man. Out of this baptism of conflict there slowly developed a new social awareness. And out of it, too, gradually evolved a democratic visual dialect as a corollary faculty. Folk experience and memory and judgment slowly yielded common perceptions, with the artist striving to assist in the selection and delimitation of data, direction of lines, and arrangement of spatial order.

From the beginning, the archaistic realism of colonial portraiture is itself not wholly to be explained by mere reference to the native distaste for 'popery,' the disapproval of fineries, or to the primitive crudeness that inheres in colonial or frontier habitations. The stiff angular poses, the metallic gleam of drapery and costume, the curious foreshortening of objects in space or foreground, the flat frontal composition, these derived only in a measure from lack of training. As much must be attributed to the theocratic setting, the extreme orthodoxy of the period. It was a foreshortened vision, bound by the restraints of an inhibiting social and religious milieu, further constricted within the cramped settlements hemmed by forest lands. The immediate concern with detail, with literal meanings, with hard, practical values, ac-companied by an unabashed scrutiny of human countenance, a scriptural assessment of character, in short, the translation of Protestantism in a materialistic setting, are reflected in colonial portraiture, the graphic counterpart of the unfolding national psychology.

If the British mode appealed to some as the ultimate refinement in portrait painting, others eschewed it for that very reason. In such a setting art itself is dandled by the finger, advertised in the newspapers among 'a choice collection of books, pictures and pickles.' [5] 'The people,' complained Copley, 'generally regard it no more than any other usefull trade'; it was a lesser craft devoted to the preservation of men's likenesses, seldom monumentally and rarely idealized. From all this, the aspiring artist intent on acquiring the requisite elegance and refinement demanded by a modish clientele could only escape for a time to Europe.

For artists visiting the Colonies the process was reversed. They were absorbed in the new environment, which already demonstrated a particular faculty for drawing fresh roots out of the transplanted European and producing hybrid blossoms and fruits peculiarly its own. The climate was especially congenial to writers like Tom Paine, Crèvecoeur, Woolman; or to painters like Smibert, Hesselius, Earl, who, breathing an atmosphere of Quakerism, instinctively discarded the Old-World Baroque as their mature style consciously regressed in fluidity and grace [6] in a deliberate preoccupation with men judged by their civic rather than financial or heraldic worth, with self-dedicated citizens of a nation born of a compelling idea rather than a homogeneous stock. And in the end, for both European and native artists who crossed and sometimes recrossed the ocean from either side, it is expressly the work done in America that yields the measure of their significance, that gives them meaning and dimension. Certain of the canvases grow subtly rich with time: the eloquent if anonymous *Elizabeth Freake with Baby Mary* in Worcester, or the *Anne Pollard* in Boston; Smibert's unforgettable *Samuel Sewall* in Boston, his *Mrs. Thomas Bull-*

[5] Quoted in Oskar Hagen, op. cit. p. 22.

[6] A thesis advanced by Alan Burroughs and further documented by Oskar Hagen; subsequently exhibited at the Rhode Island School of Design Museum.

[5]

finch in Cleveland; Badger's extraordinary *Rev. George Whitefield* at Cambridge, his *Mrs. Jonathan Edwards* in Boston; Ralph Earl's scriptural masterpiece, *Roger Sherman* at New Haven; Hesselius' *Mistress Galloway* in New York or *Mrs. Hesselius* in Philadelphia, down to Morse's *Rev. and Mrs. Bingham* in Connecticut—these may be reckoned among the great portraits.

A Master Draughtsman

IT is at once this provincialism, this prophetic fidelity to an atmosphere largely cleared of heraldic aristocracy, this fresh approach of the adolescent eye unencumbered by schools and movements, that most significantly characterizes Copley's portraiture. Benjamin Franklin pointed out that by 1750 over 90 per cent of the American population were native born, in a nation, as Edwin Hipkiss remarks, 'without fixed rank or the artificial props of primogeniture and entailed properties.'[7] That Copley painted the well-to-do, that he was himself a Tory (by circumstance rather than birth) who thought little of the mass of American people, that he scoffed at the narrow-mindedness of his townsmen and longed to get to Europe to warm his hands at the flame of the Old Masters, Raphael and Correggio, that he considered the American Revolution an act of mob violence, all this has less to do with his final product than have the spirit and the forces at work in the new land. The evidence lies in his carefully documented studies of Americans devoid of salon graces, romantic claptrap, and pretty idealization. Even when he borrows seventeenth-century drapes and colonnades, they are unadorned by lighting effects and coloristic panoply.

His are people in casual poses, nation builders and civic leaders at their desks, interrupted at their duties, or in sober Sunday best. Samuel Adams, Nathaniel Hurd, Joseph Sherburne, Mrs. Roger Morris, Joseph Barrell: they are caught in their everyday mien of sobriety, stern with themselves as with life, set for an honest walk with God, founders of the new experiment, with all the intensity of their self-dedication (Plate 3). The realism is of the mind rather than the optics, the matter-of-fact poesy of scriptural genealogy. John Foster wedded Mary Livingston and begat three sons and a daughter, each of whom is here presented in all the homeliness and 'unstooping firmness of an upright soul'[8] as revealed in the common light of day.

Later, under the influence of Smibert's properties, and in response to the gradual relaxation of Puritan codes of conduct, the importation of fineries and the liberating forces that were soon to replace the old Calvinist theology, his style develops in painterly qualities, in fluidity. His figures begin to show ease of movement as they are released in space and set, like *Mrs. Thomas Boylston* (Fogg Museum of Art) or *Mrs. Seymour Fort* (Wadsworth Atheneum), within an integrated composition; but always they retain the essential adherence to sober fact. The effigies of earlier portraitists have suddenly come to life (compare, for example, the *Thomas Amory* of Blackburn [Metcalf Collection] and of Copley [Boston]) in a portraiture such as one does not meet again elsewhere until the later nineteenth century, in Courbet and Eakins. So much of Copley is prophetic.

Yet Copley the artist had looked forward to the day when 'I shall take my flight to Europe where . . . I shall be treated with the sight of the enchanting Works of a Raphael, a Reubens, Corregio and a Veronese, etc.' The warm reception accorded his *Boy with a Squirrel*, sent to England for exhibition, West's encouraging letters, and the outbreak of the Revolution led to his departure for London (1774) where, after a two-year stay on the

[7] Edwin J. Hipkiss, *Eighteenth Century American Arts; the M. and M. Karolik Collection*, Boston, 1941, p. 11.

[8] Oskar Hagen, op. cit. p. 92.

Continent visiting Naples, Rome, Florence, Venice, he remained for the rest of his life. The traditions and atmosphere of the Old World were exhilarating. Shortly after his arrival he wrote with enthusiasm: 'I had the superlative pleasure of visiting the Royal Academy where the students had a naked model from which they were drawing.' [9] America was to wait a hundred years before such models, fully masked to dissociate their identity, could be used. To Copley it must have felt like coming home, at last. Midstream in the European tradition he hastened to acquire the polish and refinement of the new milieu. The Londoners were charmed by his ingenuous directness of approach, and for a time the spontaneous exuberance of his long cherished trip led to the painting of his finest European works. The *Brooke Watson and the Shark* (Boston), a proto-romantic treatment of a recent event, signalized Copley's interest in historical subjects of contemporary rather than remote occurrence: an extension of West's interest in historical realism.

Copley's passion for reportage, accuracy of historical detail in scenes, personages, costumes down to the last button, found full expression in a series of large canvases devoted to significant contemporary events: *The Death of the Earl of Chatham* (London), containing fifty-five portraits of which the life-size sketch (Plate 5) of the *Earl of Bathurst* (London) is a notable example; his finest historical canvas, *The Death of Major Pierson* (repelling the French at St. Heliers, Jersey, 6 January 1781) painted in 1783, was also done from an assortment of studies like that for the central group (Plate 8). Here the figures of fleeing women and children were sketched from members of Copley's own family and household. The free, nervous treatment of the escaping figures betrays one of the earliest stylistic symptoms of the romantic fever, even as the *Brooke Watson and the Shark* (Plate 7) may be said to anticipate Géricault in theme, and the drama of the entire *Major Pierson* to forecast Gros.

The style of his London portraits and conversation pieces continued for a brief period in the New England manner, but, in emulation of Old-World traditions, Copley strove for a monumentality and idealization that negated his soundest talents and vitiated his work. Faithful to what he conceived as his noblest calling, he ended as the most stilted and confused of English painters.

Waves of Influence

NO serious study has yet been accorded the basic experiences and materials by which colonial artists came to paint at all or to paint as they did. It is a phase of the total art development in the New World that merits particular stress, though it is only briefly touched upon in the following pages.

Aside from scattered examples of European woodcuts and engravings, Benjamin West's early instruction was derived from an itinerant English painter, William Williams, who also lent him Richardson's *Essays on Painting* and a translation of Dufresnoy's poem *The Art of Painting*. Significant too was the youth's deep absorption in a reading of Plutarch's *Lives*. In the Gilpin Library of the Historical Society of Pennsylvania is his sketchbook,[10] probably done during his two-and-a-half-year stay in Philadelphia (1756-9). It contains some seventy pencil drawings, among them a presumed portrait of David James Dove, the first English teacher in the Philadelphia Academy, which suggests that West also received further instruction there. Mr. Sawitzsky ascribes also some twenty paintings to West's hand in America. Since

[9] *Letters and Papers of John Singleton Copley and Henry Pelham*, 1739-1776, Massachusetts Historical Society, 1914, p. 226.

[10] Carefully described in William Sawitzsky's 'The American Work of Benjamin West,' offprint, *The Pennsylvania Magazine of History and Biography*, October 1938, p. 10.

the artist was not quite twenty-three when he left the Colonies for permanent residence abroad (1760-1820), his mature work lies outside the American tradition. From 1760-63, he traveled through Italy, carefully observing the work of the Old Masters and making large numbers of drawings, especially in Rome. By the time he reached London he had embraced the 'grand manner' and was eager to add his own contribution by way of classicism. Fascinated as he was by Greek and Roman history and myth, his work became an inspiring force, which contributed to the triumph of David, who did not hesitate to borrow subjects and motives from engravings after West's compositions.

The British had led the way in literature as in art. MacPherson's *Ossian* had arrived in 1760. A decade later West was using subjects from Spenser's *Faerie Queene*, from Shakespeare, and Saxon history. (Goethe's *Goetz von Berlichingen* [1773] was to wait for Delacroix some half-century and more later.) Throughout these works one notes a persistent overstatement, extremes of facial expression and gesture, elements implicit in both the dramaturgy of neo-classicism and the emotional excesses of romanticism. His *Death on a Pale Horse* (1802, Pennsylvania Academy), as Soby puts it, 'revives Rubens' baroque fury of movement, fiery color and turbulent conception at a time when David was still arranging his figures and furniture in an architectonic counterpoint of static and inflexible calm.' [11]

But there is a decided return to his origins in the element of realism West brought to his historical canvases—*The Death of General Wolfe* (1771, National Gallery of Canada); *Penn's Treaty with the Indians* (1772, Pennsylvania Academy; drawing in Cooper Union)—his insistence on the use of contemporary costume rather than the traditional Roman trappings. It remains his most significant innovation, borrowed with fuller documentation by Copley and further adapted to scenes of the American Revolution by Trumbull.

In his presidential 'Discourse to the Students of the Royal Academy' (1792), West spoke as an Old Master, warning the students that without a thorough knowledge of anatomy and the continual practice of drawing, 'without the execution of which I am speaking, he will find himself at last far short of the goal for which he ran, but when he is thus accomplished, nature will be sure to follow his pencil in every line. . .'

His own drawings are a measure of his wide-ranging interests. The *Figure Composition* (Plate 12) is Italianate; the broken line of the *Dr. Bragg* (Plate 11) suggests the Dutch School and a touch of Rembrandt; the *Head of an Old Man* (Plate 9) in spirit and execution is largely derived from Rubens; while the *Three Sisters* (Plate 13) breathes the sentimental grace that later appealed to the Pre-Raphaelites.

Such was the variety of drawings and paintings that three generations of American artists, Benbridge, Pratt, Delaney, Brown, Copley, Peale, Stuart, Sully, Allston, Dunlap, Earl, Waldo, Fulton, Morse, Malbone, and a dozen others, came to study and absorb, imitate and discard. And as the historical themes were inspiration for Trumbull's lifework, and the portraiture for that of Pratt and Sully, so the example and appeal of the romantic subjects struck a responsive chord in Allston and Morse. West's influence on these visiting fellow countrymen was enormous and in this lies his primary significance, in his personal qualities and his contact with a host of American students to whom his London studio was a refuge, a retreat from the indifference of the home folks. Here was guidance, instruction, even monetary aid; here was studio life and aesthetic 'high seriousness'; here was the example of a kindly and sympathetic master, an outstanding leader of the British School; thoroughly absorbed in and devoted to the art life, to scholarship and experiment, to technical knowledge and skill; not very talkative or even well-spoken, but glowing with enthusiasms and, like the true pedagogue, with catholic tastes and a ready championship of whatever seemed worthy of emulation. By the same token the bulk of his own work is largely derivative, his canvases, always ambitious, mirror his enthusiasms but remain pedantic in all aspects save occasionally that of composition. He had himself warned his students: 'The young artist . . . who is seduced by examples from originality in that which he had embraced as his forte, can never be great.' If his technical facility rendered him a superb copyist, his original

[11] James T. Soby, *Romantic Painting in America*, New York, 1943.

work remains for the most part a distinct echo of intermingled voices of the past. But as the Dean of American painters, West was first adored, then venerated, by three generations of art students who throve on his sympathy and kindliness, his perceptive criticism, and generous praise. In them he instilled a full appreciation of the importance of drawing, kindling new enthusiasms, widening their horizons, training their eyes, and giving them a vision of the great tradition that left them forever dissatisfied with mere portraiture or the ready facility of routine patterns and formulas. It was a vision they carried with them and strove breathlessly to express when they reached home again. For them there could be no return to smugness and provincialism. They might, like Stuart and Malbone, follow their own stylistic bent, but art for all of them became a solemn dedication and a way of life.

Before his departure for England, John Trumbull, a prize Latin scholar, listed sixty-eight of his own drawings and paintings [12] done after prints, other oil copies, and plates in the *Gentleman's Magazine*, including subjects like *Brutus Condemning His Sons; Belisarius* (from Strange's engraving after Salvatore Rosa); *A Nun by Candlelight,* etc. As a student of West in London, Trumbull devoted himself assiduously to anatomical and life studies (Plate 17), and it was only later that, intent on a thorough application of spot realism, he made energetic trips to scenes of contemporary action, visiting the homes of participants, to sketch the materials and portraits of his historical canvases.

Trumbull entered Harvard college at fifteen with a particular gift for drawing. A brilliant student, bored by college studies, he absorbed Hogarth's *Analysis of Beauty.* Securing a copy of the work of the mathematician Dr. Brook Taylor, *Jesuit's Perspective,* he devoted a drawing book to copying its intricate diagrams. At Copley's house in Cambridge he saw real paintings for the first time. A collection of Piranesi's prints further inflamed his desire to draw and paint. His brief military career as a colonel in the Revolutionary War and second aide-de-camp to General Washington enabled him to do spot drawings of maneuvers and general army

[12] John Trumbull, *Autobiography, Reminiscences and Letters,* New York, 1841, p. 59 ff.

life (Plate 18). Out of the army, he rented Smibert's old study and resumed work.

Despite the admonition of his father, then Governor of Connecticut, Trumbull escaped to England and West's studio. Sensible of the superb import of the historical events of his own lifetime, he there later determined, as he wrote Jefferson, to dedicate his life 'to preserve and diffuse the memory of the noblest actions; to impart to future generations the glorious lessons of human rights, and of the spirit with which these should be asserted and supported. . .' [13]

Imprisoned in retaliation for the seizure and execution of Major André in America, and ordered home upon his release, the student traveled via Dover, Amsterdam, and Bilboa, doing a series of delicate landscape drawings that reflect an orderly mind, intent upon the facts of each scene scaled down to pleasing intervals of linear rhythm in proper application of Taylor's laws of perspective. Even the tumultuous *Niagara,* done later, of which two paintings are in the Wadsworth Atheneum, is largely a documentary record of fact soberly reduced to scale. Trumbull doubtless recognized that his gift was for literal recording rather than flights of imaginative fancy, the classicism of *Officers Crying* (Plate 19), or romantic themes from Shakespeare. Upon his return to West's studio four years later, he decided upon his visual history of the American Revolution.

An aristocrat by instinct and training, like Hamilton he scoffed at the Republic, yet like him was nevertheless aware of the historic necessity of the Revolution. An exceptional draughtsman with considerable study and practice at the Academy life classes, steeped in the tradition of the Old Masters, highly inventive in composition, he possessed the necessary practical skill and more than sufficient zeal for the task. As researcher and historian in paint, his prime interest was always in the *realia* of the moment. Trumbull toured the country to gather sketches of the actual settings and costumes, making notes of eyewitness accounts and innumerable portrait sketches as working models. As a scholar in paint, he composed his tableaux with conscientious fidelity to detail. His *Battle of Bunker's Hill* drew its inspiration from West's *Death of General Wolfe,* while his *Death*

[13] Ibid. p. 158.

of General Montgomery (New Haven, Connecticut) bears a direct kinship to Copley's *Death of Major Pierson.* The most original and by far the most painterly of his canvases, the *Sortie from Gibraltar* (Cincinnati, Ohio), has a formal and static correctness that betrays little personal temperament or verve. His best work is to be found in the intimacy and delicate draughtsmanship of his miniatures and occasional sketches.

It was Charles Willson Peale who assumed Copley's role as chief portraitist upon the latter's departure from Boston. A Captain of the Volunteers in the Revolution, he was at various times and together saddlemaker, clockmaker, dental mechanic, silversmith, politician, naturalist, lecturer, showman, founder of the old Museum of Natural History, and of the Pennsylvania Academy of the Fine Arts. Early in his career he happened across the technical *Handmaid to the Arts,* anonymously published by Robert Dossie (1764), and abruptly decided to become an artist. His first attempt, with paints and brushes secured from a coachmaker, was a landscape. After some lessons with John Hesselius, at twenty-four he went up to Boston where he visited Smibert's studio and presumably took brief instruction from Copley, whose fame had already spread. After two years in London,

and with every prospect of a successful career, he returned to aid the Revolution. While taking part in the battles of Trenton and Germantown, as Tuckerman says, he 'sedulously improved his leisure by sketching from nature,' producing as well some forty portrait miniatures painted during the critical winter at Valley Forge. His troops had faced the British between the Schuylkill and the Brandywine and along the latter he did a series of extraordinarily sensitive sketches dated 1777 (Plate 15).

Like Copley, West, and Trumbull, Peale was essentially a draughtsman whose work loses little in reproduction and often improves with the elimination of spotty or lurid coloring. Even in the *Staircase Group* (Philadelphia Museum) and *Family Group* (New York Historical Society) his designs are essentially linear, and he rarely attempts aerial composition or color design in perspective. He is the first thoroughly American craftsman, devoted to a sane, homely realism in his portraits, built up, like the *Benjamin Franklin* (Pennsylvania Academy) with a carefully selected enumeration of pointed detail. It is a kind of shirt-sleeve workmanship with the highest point of intensity centered on the face of the sitter.

End of an Era

WEST tried with little success to get Gilbert Stuart to attend the Royal Academy School. Devoted to the larger issues of oil technique, Stuart recognized that his gift for flesh painting could only be stayed in its flash and spontaneity by painstaking considerations of drawing. 'Drawing the features distinctly and carefully in chalk,' he told Jouett, 'is a loss of time. All studies should be made with brush in hand. It is nonsense to think of perfecting onself in drawing before one begins to paint.' [14] Yet, when Trumbull was quoted as

saying that Stuart 'never could exercise the patience necessary to correct drawing,' [15] Stuart's friend Waterhouse, with whom he had visited picture collections in England once a week for two years, retorted that Stuart 'was patient and even laborious in his drawings'; [16] and Jane Stuart later wrote Dunlap: 'I believe he thought it impossible for one to be an artist without acquiring a thorough

Harris Jouett from conversations with Gilbert Stuart in 1816, New York, 1939, p. 85.

[15] William Dunlap, *History . . . of the Arts of Design,* revised by F. W. Bayley and C. E. Goodspeed, Boston, 1918, vol. II, p. 210.

[16] Ibid. p. 210.

[14] John Hill Morgan, *Gilbert Stuart and His Pupils;* together with the complete notes on painting by Matthew

knowledge of drawing and anatomy, and he certainly gave a great deal of time to these studies in earlier years.'[17] Elsewhere she wrote that he 'attended the discourses of Sir Joshua Reynolds on painting and those of Mr. Cruikshank on anatomy, drawing in the evening in the life school and painting with his master.' Of this there is little recorded evidence, but that Stuart could 'draw with the brush,' securing his lines of definition and contour and building up certain plastic values in color, goes without saying. That he could use the pen with great assurance, the alleged *Self Portrait*[18] (Plate 14) scratched on the back of a letter, now lost but reproduced from an etched version by James Duthie in Mason's *Life of Stuart*, would appear to demonstrate.[19]

Association with the visiting Scotch portraitist Cosmo Alexander resulted in a trip to Edinburgh and then to London and West's studio. But Stuart wanted little of West's academism. 'For my own part,' he insisted, 'I will not follow any master. I wish to find out what nature is for myself, and see her with my own eyes.'[20] It is an attitude that recurs with such frequency, from Malbone to Winslow Homer, as to suggest a national habit of mind. For the rest, Stuart's talents and tastes ran to the cultured and aristocratic abroad, where his success was immediately assured.

At home, that segment of the native population which before the Revolution and after had found it expedient to quit the country, took with it a good deal of the Old-World culture and refinement, leaving a social residue that already strained in the direction of Jacksonianism. Stunned by the shock of separation, New England had lain fallow, incapable of an original idea; though signficantly, the generation born between 1803-19, from Emerson and Thoreau to Hawthorne, Melville, and Whitman, was to produce the great body of American letters. But these men were still to come, or were yet in swaddling clothes. Meantime, as if to demonstrate to America the way that it had gone, to point up the essential difference in temper and psychology that set off America from the preoccupations of the mother country, Stuart returned after some eighteen years' absence, almost a foreigner. Coming upon the fallow ground of New England out of the most fashionable British circles, for a time he alternately scandalized and salved the wounds of the remnant *elite* guard. At a time when, for Americans, going to England was no longer, as Dunlap explained, 'going home'; when it was no longer indispensable to make the grand tour with half an eye to a salon portrait done in the academy district; when a new crop of well-to-do succeeding upon the old showed itself eager for some participation in the fading transplanted culture; at this time Stuart offered a final opportunity to be painted in the classic Georgian manner. Here was a monumental style set for posterity. Eschewing the everyday, the accidence of the moment, it highlighted in vibrant tones the distinguished aspects of men and women. Concentrating always on aristocratic features in their best attitudes, Stuart keyed his palette to the flow and moistness of living flesh, and with a loose, shimmering brushwork produced a eulogizing portraiture that, except rarely as in the early *Dr. Benjamin Waterhouse* (Newport, Massachusetts), and the *James Ward* (Minneapolis), and some of the post-European portraits beginning with *Mrs. Yates* (Washington, D. C.), or the *Nathaniel Bowditch*, (J. H. Bowditch collection), lacks the substructure of bone, sinew, and nerve. The perspective of two centuries allows us to stretch a line of characteristic continuity across the total American art production. That line clearly omits most of Stuart's work, which was at once the epitome and the grand finale of a tradition that had come to the astonishing realization that it was alien in the New World.

Alan Burroughs points out that while Stuart 'was making aristocratic portraits, Chester Harding and Francis Alexander [both self-taught itinerants] were making plain, blunt likenesses in the democratic spirit, and rivaling Stuart in Boston without the aid of his brilliant technique.'[21] They were considerably busier and more productive than Stuart because, as Harding explains, of 'the cir-

[17] George C. Mason, *Life and Works of Gilbert Stuart*, New York, 1879, vol. 1, pp. 39-40.

[18] Ascribed to Stuart in Henry Tuckerman's *Book of the Artists*, New York, 1867, p. 111.

[19] Jouett, op. cit. p. 83, quotes Stuart as saying: 'Be decisive in your drawing. . . I owe half my success to this.'

[20] Reported by Neagle in Dunlap, op. cit. vol. i, p. 216.

[21] Alan Burroughs, *Limners and Likenesses*, Cambridge, 1936, p. 104.

cumstances of my being a backwoodsman, newly caught; then the circumstance of my being self-taught was trumpeted about much to my advantage.' [22] Here was obviously another class of people, motivated by other ideals, whose voice was more insistently heard. By such means, and by basking in the more congenial light of French Republican portraiture, in the work of Vanderlyn, Morse, Rembrandt Peale, Robert Fulton, and others, rather than by Stuart's chromotechnics, did native portraiture seek to grow its own roots.

The key to Sully's endeavor lies in the description of his meeting with Stuart in 1807, when the young artist was twenty-four: 'I had the privilege of standing by the artist's chair during the sitting [of Andrew Allen, his friend] a situation I valued more at that moment than I shall ever again appreciate any station on earth.' [23]

His particular talent, that of delineating the charm and modish grace of women, earned him proud comparison with Sir Thomas Lawrence, but the dominant influence throughout is that of Stuart. The fragile assurance of his line and wash drawings (Plates 28, 30) suggests the direct means by which he captured the physical and psychological bearing of these gentle creatures who display an elegant sweep of shoulders, a witchery of wasp waists, that mark the full flowering of the cult of femininity. Stuart remarked that if Sully had been able to stay on in England an additional two years, he would have risen to the top of his profession in America. And ended, one might add, as alien to the native school as Stuart. As it is, the famous *Boy with a Torn Hat* (Boston), for example, is as thoroughly in the British tradition as his *Queen Victoria* (Metropolitan Museum). Only occasionally is an element of native distinction attached to his portraits. A fusion of sense and sensibility, these creatures are still close enough to Quaker precepts to avoid simpering elegance; in the best of them, *Mrs. Chamberlain* (H. L. Pratt Collection), *Miss Rebecca Gratz* (Collection Miss Henrietta Clay), *Sarah Sully* (San Antonio, Texas), a wholesomeness and an open, alert intelligence suggest that the pioneer is not very far removed.

[22] Chester Harding, quoted in Dunlap, op. cit. vol. III, p. 68.

[23] Ibid. vol. II, p. 237.

Stuart's influence and advice were equally marked in the career of John Neagle, who endeavored to surpass the work of his father-in-law, Thomas Sully, in attainment of coloristic sophistication and refinement of style. Early study with an immigrant Italian drawing master, Pietre Ancora, gave him a taste for careful construction that was enhanced by a strong sense of design, derived from subsequent apprenticeship to a coach and ornamental painter. At nineteen, Neagle entered the studio of the portraitist Otis Bass, who was then busy with engraving and lithography. There followed a brief period of wandering in search of work, after which he returned to his mother's house in Philadelphia, where he set up as portrait painter.

The dilemma of opposing points of view and compulsions is subtly projected in much of Neagle's work. While, like Sully, he bent every effort of will to acquire the salon graces, his instinct for accuracy and a homespun genre quality regularly interposed in such superior portraits as that of *Mr. Reilly* (Minneapolis). For his *Pat Lyons at His Forge* (Pennsylvania Academy), he measured and carefully drew all objects in the smithy, as eager to secure vigorous and faithful representation as to achieve style. His realistic concern with a detailed approach marks his essential difference from Sully. Time and again the burr of his native idiom gives way to the resonant cadences of British parlor conversation, his careful line seeking, not always with the assurance of Sully, the elegance and poise that link with the British tradition. But it was the genre element, like that in the study of his famous blacksmith, monumentally presented in the posture and attitude of a fellow who can, whenever he desires, leave his shop to drink and sup with any man, that meant so much to another artist, Caleb Bingham, who later came up out of the West looking for direction and guidance in Philadelphia.

Conclusion

In a nation whose political arena was so perennially crowded with a succession of embattled giants fighting the good cause, where the cleavage of opinion in the grandstands was so vociferous and desperately loyal, when every lesser issue of the day was wrangled over cracker barrels and teacups, one wonders that so little of it all appeared in the art of the day. One is prone to note the Georgian eulogizers and epitaphers and conclude that nothing truly native emerged before the crucible of civil war fused the national character and the artist appeared at last an an adult participant.

Yet, if we look carefully, we shall find that our earlier artists spoke by indirection, through choice of image that, consciously or not, carried their more profound convictions. By implication rather than explication, Bunker Hill and the Declaration of Independence are recorded more truly in Copley, Earl, Feke, C. W. Peale, and Neagle than in Trumbull's paintings of those events. The selection of facial contours, the choice of documentary details, the insistence on democratic prose, the bill-of-rights concern with the ordinary man, represent the tacit but full expression of the artist's social function.

American Romanticism

NEITHER paradox nor bias of thesis is alone responsible for the fact that studies of Realism and of Romanticism in American painting cull their illustrative examples from the works of the same artists and often the identical paintings, from Copley's *Brooke Watson and the Shark*, West's *Death of General Wolfe*, Trumbull's *Sortie*, to Winslow Homer's and Thomas Benton's work. Both elements run parallel, or in alternate periods of youth and maturity, in the work of most individual artists and frequently mingle in a single work, where mood and viewpoint may be largely of one nature, and technique of handling of another. Implicit is something of the androgynous nature of the 'lyrical ballads,' comprising on the one hand poetry devoted to the everyday people, language, and scenes over which is thrown a rich coloring of the imagination; and on the other, themes concerned with the highly improbable rendered probable and close at hand. (Thus in painting, the 'magic realism' of fantasy is made secure by perdurable realistic handling.) In American art particularly, romantic realism, or romantic naturalism alternated with sober fancy. For the American dream was rooted in pragmatism, and appropriately the very literalness of American painting, the forthright and homely presentation of men and manners, inevitably carried overtones of purest Romanticism. Constance Rourke has it that: 'Woven into all our folklore is an acute observa-

tion of the external world . . . and this tends to be poetic rather than naturalistic. . . Indeed, a full knowledge of our folklore and folk-song would reveal the subordinate place that naturalism constantly took in our early free expression.' [24]

America itself remained a major symbol and canon in the Romantic doctrine; she alone afforded the true background for the liberating energies, the proper soil on which might flourish the innate goodness of man. But in America, where pragmatism was to run its full and ultimate course, Romanticism cast a peculiar glow of magic for a brief time [25] and then subsided, only to reappear in the work of scattered artists like Blakelock,

[24] Constance Rourke, op. cit. p. 293.

[25] In Europe, Romanticism was a way of life, a philosophic creed, a literary manifesto and a method of revolt. In painting it left its mark on the style, the coloration, the composition and design, the very drawing. But artists like Morse and Inman returning from Europe felt little impulse or encouragement to continue their romantic scenes. In America there was neither stylistic reaction nor social and political revolt; the young nation still held thrilling promise of fulfilment of the Romantic ideals. Extremes of Romanticism were easily tempered by the Yankee head on Greek shoulders. Faced with the crass necessities of earning a living, artists like Peale, Morse, Fulton, Bingham, exploited all their talents for enterprise, politics, practical affairs, as well as the arts, devoting head and hand to one, while the heart and spirit moved with the other. They were all one with Bryant who left his heart in the New England landscape and moved on to a practical career in New York.

Quidor, Ryder, Eilshemius—solitaries associated with no school or movement.

The single figure most readily identifiable with the European Romantic movement both in his person and his work, Washington Allston, like his friend Coleridge, produced few great works among a scattered abundance of preparatory sketches. A lover of music, class poet at Harvard, a brilliant, handsome youth, who was carried to Europe by the full sweep of the Romantic tide, he thought to embrace its turbulence and color, and like Irving, Prescott, and later, Longfellow, to bring back to America something of Old-World culture. Not alone in theme, but in conception, design, handling of color in canvases like *The Deluge* (Metropolitan Museum) and *Moonlit Landscape* (Boston), similar to the sketch (Plate 25), Allston painted as he lived, romantically. The spirit and temper of the romantic were native to his blood: one who could dream of the most ravishing of women, dreams that left him 'in a state of quiet ethereal exaltation' [26] for days, haunted by the vision for months; or who, for unaccountable reasons, and to the dismay of his friends, destroyed 'the finest head I ever painted,' the *Agony of Judas;* who, after a brilliant career in Europe, discovered on his return to America in 1818 that he 'had returned to a mighty empire,' only to stay on a respected but tragic figure, vaporizing in the effete intellectual atmosphere of Cambridge, between two worlds, one dead, the other yet unborn.

Emerson was to speak of America as a 'country of beginnings, of projects, of vast designs and expectations. It has no past: all has an onward and prospective look.' [27] But for Allston the years brought only disillusion and inexplicable frustration. In the face of so vast a design, so big with promise, yet so non-romantic in its materialism, so foreboding in its local symptoms, the artist's talents were immobilized. America's sweetest dream had

for the moment turned nightmare: the vaunted frontier life and pioneer spirit so widely poetized, heralding the recovery of man's true nobility, had become in actuality an adventure of the pioneer that was marked by 'sadisms and masochisms,' by 'bestial swilling and bullying.' [28] Lewis Mumford adds: 'Instead of seeking nature in a wise passiveness, as Wordsworth urged, he raped his new mistress in a blind fury of obstreperous passion. . . The truth is that the life of the pioneer was bare and insufficient; he did not really face nature, he merely evaded society.' [29]

In the end, Romanticism itself had backfired. The excesses were not an isolated experience. The surging tide of bitter disillusion welled back among the urban centers and was briefly echoed in the melancholy fascination of Poe's morbidity, in the enormous popularity with which Rembrandt Peale's traveling exhibition of *The Court of Death* (Detroit) was everywhere received. Allston spent the best part of his mature years struggling with his huge canvas, the *Feast of Belshazaar* (Boston), forever erasing, somehow incapable of composing and completing the scene depicting 'the handwriting on the wall.' In a nation happily intent on 'making things work,' romantics like Allston, Morse, Cole, could only remark with Hunt that 'In another country I might have been a painter'; and seek refuge in the consolatory remark of Inman that: 'The business of a few generations of painters in this country as in all others, is to prepare the way for their successors.' In the larger sense, as artists they may be said to have failed magnificently, unable to fuse the diverging national traditions, relinquishing their European laurels in order to return home and enrich the native grounds for indigenous seedlings—romantic and lyric realists.

[26] Jared B. Flagg, *The Life and Letters of Washington Allston*, New York, 1892, p. 8 *et passim.*

[27] Ibid. p. 140.

[28] Quoted in Lewis Mumford's *The Golden Day*, New York, 1926, p. 89, and pp. 79-80. The idea is earlier expressed in Henry Adams' *History of the United States, during the Administrations of Jefferson and Madison,* 1889-91.

[29] Ibid. p. 59.

Schools, Books, and Methods

ALLSTON'S introduction to art had followed the usual pattern. In a Charleston library as a lad he had seen engravings from Boydell's Shakespeare Gallery and was fascinated by Fuseli's illustration for the Ghost Scene in *Hamlet*. Later: 'My chief pleasure now was in drawing from prints, of all kinds of figures, landscapes, animals.' [30] He was soon making romantic illustrations of his own, the *Storming of Roderick's Castle*, etc. On a visit to New York and in need of encouragement, he often visited the shop of a Mr. King, an occasional portraitist. Malbone, too, lent him drawings; and, determined to advance their art, together they left for England in 1801. Of his first meeting with West, Allston wrote: 'I shall never forget his benevolent smile when he took me by the hand . . .' and, seeing his gallery, 'I pronounced him one of the greatest men in the world.' And so Allston, like his predecessors, at the instance of West, was enrolled in the Royal Academy.

Such in brief was to be the recurring pattern of experience for American artists before mid-nineteenth century: early contact with prints and drawing books, brief guidance at home, for some a period of training at West's studio or the Royal Academy Schools, the grand tour, the return home, often to an indifferent public. However, returning artists like Peale (founder of the Pennsylvania Academy), Trumbull (American Academy), Morse (National Academy), Allston, brought with them a heightened, if academic, notion of the vital role that drawing played in design, structure, and modeling. They gave that role a timely emphasis that now drew the attention of younger artists who, having been exclusively preoccupied with color portraiture, were coming to feel with Allston

that the majority of London portraitists were 'the damnedest stupid wretches that ever disgraced a profession.' That remark signalized the end of an era, and opportunely the returning veterans brought home the realization that painting required a thorough knowledge of compositional drawing.

A typical letter of Allston's to a young artist reads:

I should warmly recommend your devoting a portion of every day to drawing; for this reason, that if an artist does not acquire a correct design *while young,* he never will. . . A painter may be blessed with every gift of nature but unless he has acquired the art of design he can never *express himself.* If you would not be tormented by a consciousness of having noble and beautiful conceptions to which you cannot give birth, you must give much of your time to drawing. . . My own practice is to make a finished outline always before touching the brush to canvas.

Elsewhere, '. . . the pencil is in my hand daily, and excepting the Sabbath, or when precluded by business, has been for years.' [31] To John Greenough, 'I am delighted to hear that you are devoting your time to drawing. No reputation, however high during the artist's life . . . ,' et cetera. It is advice reiterated with the frequency of admonition—a solemn warning.

In America, drawing as such had been no novelty. Scores of eighteenth-century manuals were available in England and the Continent, of which numbers, like Brook Taylor's *Jesuit's Perspective* or Dossie's *Handmaid of the Arts,* doubtless made their way across the Atlantic. Popular titles ran into several editions: Peacham's *The Compleat Gentleman . . .* to which is added the Gentle-

[30] Jared B. Flagg, op. cit. p. 8 ff.

[31] Ibid. p. 287.

man's exercise, or, an exquisite practice, as well for drawing all manner of beasts, as for making colors, to be used in painting, limning . . . (reissued 1612-61); *The Ladies Amusement* (London, 1770's); Carington Bowles' *All Draughtsmen's Assistant* (London, 1777); a volume by Lairesse (Amsterdam, 1727); a French volume by A. A. Jombert (1740). Beginning with the first years of the nineteenth century, American drawing manuals and 'instructors' were published in quantity, adaptations of European books and new titles, with improvements, appearing annually and winning amateur converts everywhere.[32]

Earl's *Portrait of William Taylor* (dated 1790, Albright Gallery, Buffalo) shows the gentleman as an amateur artist engaged on a chalk drawing of the landscape view from his own window. The practice of making sketching trips to the countryside was recommended by Edward Dayes in his . . . *Excursions through the principal parts of Derbyshire and Yorkshire* . . . with Instructions for Drawing and Colouring Landscapes (1805). This was echoed in William Charles' *A Drawing Book of Rural Scenery* (Philadelphia, 1814), illustrated with views clearly English. There appeared the widely popular *Progressive Drawing Book* by Lucas Fielding, Jr. (Baltimore, 1827-8), fully illustrated with local scenes (pseudo-local in manner) done by Latrobe. A quantity of drawing books, foreign and local, swept the country in the late 1830's. By the middle of the century, drawing had become part of the public-school curriculum,[33] vying with physical training as a molder of character and refinement. Quoting Goethe's 'We talk too much and draw too little,' Rembrandt Peale, professor of Graphics in the Central High School of Philadelphia, published his *Graphics* in 1838, a manual that was officially adopted by the City School Board. The book was reissued as late as 1845. Two years later J. G. Chapman, who had

decorated a panel of the rotunda in the Capitol, published his excellent *Amateur's Drawing Manual*, enumerating the delights as well as profits that await all who 'may be safely invited and tempted to the study of drawing.'

With all this, opportunities for professional instruction remained meager. In Boston of 1748 Peter Pelham had briefly taught drawing and 'the art of painting on glass.' From 1763-8 John Durand, with modest claims of ability, advertised a Drawing School at Broad Street in New York.[34] In 1792, Archibald Robertson,[35] the Scottish painter who had done a portrait of Washington, founded one of the first academies in America at 89 William Street in New York. It was attended in his spare time by John Vanderlyn, while he worked for Thomas Barrow, an English dealer in prints then established in New York.

Young Dunlap, when he injured his eye in a game and was confined to bed, found in his father's library Hogarth's illustrations of Butler's *Hudibras*, and Taylor's *Life of Christ* with plates, which he copied in India ink. Later, wishing to study art, he was taken, about 1778, to Mr. Ramage 'in reality the only artist in New York.' But as this artist was too busy to undertake tutoring, Dunlap was taken to one William Williams, 'to his rooms in the suburbs, now Mott Street, and he placed a drawing book before me, such as I had possessed for years: after a few visits the teacher was not to be found. I examined his portraits—tried his crayons, and soon procuring a set, commenced painting portraits, beginning with my father's.'[36]

Such was the recurring experience. Stray visiting artists and odd settlers in the main centers—Smibert, Pelham, Blackburn, Williams, Ancora, Alexander, Robertson—served to guide the initial footsteps until the youngsters could get to West's studio or the Continent. In the outlying regions, typical tales are those of West or Malbone, making their own brushes and colors; Peale, borrowing

[32] Carl W. Dreppard, *American Drawing Books*, Bulletin of the New York Public Library, vol. 49, no. 11, November 1945, pp. 795-812. Cf. also Ch. III in his *American Pioneer Arts and Artists*, Springfield, Mass., 1942.

[33] 'Drawing has recently been admitted into the school curriculum and, as education here is the same for all classes of people, it is to be hoped that the taste for painting will become universal.' Cf. Avrahm Yarmolinsky, *Picturesque United States of America*, 1811-1813, Being a Memoir on Paul Svinin, New York, 1930, p. 38.

[34] Cf. William Kelby, *Notes on American Artists*, 1754-1820, copied from advertisements in newspapers, New York, 1922.

[35] A. Robertson, in *Elements of the Graphic Arts*, New York, 1802, p. 10, recommended to his students three European books: Mason's translation of Du Fresnay's *de Arte Graphica*, Gelphin's *Essays on Landscape Painting*, and Price's *Landscape Painting*.

[36] Dunlap, op. cit. vol. I, p. 296.

materials from a coach painter; or Francis Alexander, who at twenty thought the local shop signs of Providence represented the ultimate in painting.

The day was to come when the academies founded by Peale, Trumbull, and Morse would offer some systematic direction, when drawing classes like that of Hunt in Boston, and schools and societies (The New York Academy, the Apollo Association, the Sketch Club, the Art-Union), would come to life for a brief but illuminating period, when exhibitions would spring up and flourish in a score of communities, and artists would make their appearance ever westward, the paint brush always following 'hard upon the rifle.'

Meantime the native artists had to discover what painting was. In the absence of a common body of technical fundamentals, without the aid of an art tradition, academies, galleries, exhibitions, or standards of criticism, they had to find their own way, often in the face of poverty and public neglect. And coming, as it were, piecemeal upon the knowledge of softening paints, of mixing colors, of preparing canvases, sizing, glazing, scumbling, of shading and tinting, and reproducing the human features, of composing groups and creating space, they treasured it as a precious body of skills. In London, Copley gathered up every new-found technical discovery and promptly reported it in letters to his stepbrother Henry Pelham. Sully took great pains to write out the methods and materials of the craft in his *Hints to Painters*, as did Neagle in his *Commonplace Book*. One of the very few who really glimpsed the meaning of the Old Masters, Allston studied the painter's craft with scholarly devotion, was meticulous in his use of paints and glazes, and made detailed descriptive notes of his methods, as did Stuart through conversations with Jouett.

If all this technical information was but slowly disseminated in America, the country, nevertheless, as one visitor put it, 'seemed to swarm with painters.' Public taste was literal and naive rather than perceptive and sympathetic, and it did not hesitate to express its preferences. Dunlap says that Stuart complained that local criticism was 'too nice and exacted too much.' 'In England my efforts were compared with those of Vandyck, Titian and other great painters, but here they

compared them with the works of the Almighty.' [37] At least they were on the right track, with technical knowledge, stylistic traditions, and a slowly mounting public interest. By 1834 Dunlap had published his informative *Rise and Progress of the Arts of Design in America;* the first version of Tuckerman's encyclopedic *Book of the Artists* appeared in 1848.

With all this, there could be precious little of dandyism and dilettantism in America. The struggle was too costly, the rewards too moderate; the challenge of the Old Masters and the ideal of achievement they set were too real, the climate of opinion too pragmatic to attract the lily-wristed aesthete. On the contrary, a high seriousness, embarrassing at times in its intensity of resolve and aspiration, marks the endeavor of American artists. Copley apologized to Liotard, the Swiss pastelist, that 'it is not for want of inclination' that paintings in America are not better. It drove him from mere successful portraiture to moral allegories and historical dramas, which, while they ruined him artistically and financially, remain as monuments to his integrity, however mistaken. West similarly scorned salon portraiture for grand moral canvases, a giant of eclecticism whom time alone has reduced to minor stature. Trumbull was content with nothing less than the epochal events of the Revolution. Malbone, exercising his rich but particular talents in miniature painting, drove himself to an early death of unswerving labors. In London, Sully seriously impaired his eyes studying anatomy by candlelight far into the night.

The chronicle hardly varies. Mather Brown had gone to England with a chip on his shoulder: 'I will let them see if an obscure Yankee boy cannot shine as great as any of them.' Caleb Bingham walked about 'whispering sometimes to myself that in the familiar line which I have chosen, I am the greatest among all the disciples of the brush, which my native land has yet produced.[38] Winslow Homer as a lad looked at a canvas by Frère and remarked that he wished to paint 'something like that, only a damned sight better.' A superb conviction, almost a divine self-assurance animates these men. 'You have talents,' writes Allston to

[37] William T. Whitley, *Gilbert Stuart*, Cambridge, 1932, p. 89.

[38] Albert Christ-Janer, *George Caleb Bingham*, New York, 1940, p. 77.

Charles Frazer, the best miniaturist of the South, 'cultivate them—and it is not impossible that the name Frazer may one day be as celebrated as those of Raphael and Michel Angelo.'[39] And Morse writes his mother, '. . . had I no higher thoughts than being a portrait painter I would have chosen a far different profession. My ambition is to be among those who shall revive the splendor of the fifteenth century, to rival the genius of a Raphael, a Michel Angelo, or a Titian. . .'[40]

Men, Manners, and Landscape

DISSATISFACTION with 'mere portraiture' had been manifested not only by the painters, but by the colonists themselves, who were not always happy with the neo-classic drapes and colonnades frequently inserted as background. In keeping with the widespread taste for local topographical views, merchants preferred glimpses of trees or harbor views as decorative notes in their portraits. Such embellishment was easily supplied by copying or borrowing from Italian or Dutch prints. Thus we find Smibert in 1744 ordering a set of prints of ships, explaining, 'These ships I want sometimes for to be in a distant view in Portraits of Merchts etc. who chuse such. . .'[41] Other touches appeared in Feke's (?) *Oxenbridge Thacher* (A. G. Thacher Collection), in Blackburn's *Theodore Atkinson, Jr.* (Providence, Rhode Island) and *The Bowdoin Children* (Bowdoin, Maine), in Copley's *Mr. and Mrs. Ralph Izard* (Boston). But the real challenge to the artists remained. Rather than some ill-sorted, foreign scene, the merchant or landowner naturally hankered to have the delightful vista of his own farm or estate worked in as backdrop for his worthy self. The lost 'landskips' of Smibert and Theus may well have been adaptations of local scenes in the manner of the European prints they had used. The window views in half the portraits painted by Ralph Earl, the panoramic views of his native town *Looking East*

from Leicester Hills (1800, Worcester Art Museum) and those of Francis Guy, a visiting Englishman, represent the clearest development of this trend to estate portraiture. Few artists were yet capable of handling the theme, but by 1800 converging forces tended to direct the attention of the younger men to landscape painting for its own sake, unadorned by portraiture or historical interest.

With autonomy achieved, a renewed self-confidence was inspired by the formal establishment of a people's government set within a framework of democratic processes. The young nation moved on to economic independence as a resurgence of full-blown nationalism acclaimed the end of the War of 1812. Both events contributed to the comfortable attitude of a people who, having subdued their environment, could pause to admire the greater handiwork of nature. America was now rediscovered by its natives, who brought to it the Romantic mood if not the license of the European movement. In England that mood had been largely literary and moralizing. Newton's 'nature methodized,' reflected in Poussin as in Alexander Pope, had yielded to a nature sentimentalized in Thompson's 'Seasons' and Young's melancholy 'Night Thoughts.' Wordsworth's 'Intimations' and 'Preludes,' Coleridge's popular 'He prayeth best,' were echoed in American Transcendentalism, and Emerson's *Essay on Nature* proclaimed the immanence of God in Nature and man's duty to seek spiritual harmony with both.

In American art, the earlier emphasis on man and his immediate destiny, the interest in the Founders and makers, gave way to a concern with man's habitat. Crèvecoeur, Freneau, Bryant had

[39] Jared B. Flagg, op. cit. p. 47.

[40] Harry B. Wehle, *S. F. B. Morse*, Metropolitan Museum Exhibition Catalogue, New York, 1932, p. 7. For the full correspondence, cf. E. L. Morse, *S. F. B. Morse*, Letters and Journals, Boston, 1914, vol. i, p. 102 ff.

[41] *Proceedings of the Massachusetts Historical Society*, October 1915, pp. 30-31.

marveled at the vastness, the immemorial splendor of the virgin lands 'never deformed by culture.' Trumbull had nodded acknowledgment in his Niagara views. Allston's extraordinary *Elijah Fed by the Ravens* (Boston) carried landscape into the realm of the purely imaginative and febrile, responding to the mood of Coleridge's 'Xanadu' as had the Venetians to the bucolic idylls of Sannazaro. Peale had sketched along the Brandywine. Neagle painted along the Schuylkill, as did Birch, Jarvis, and Sully. By 1820 Thomas Doughty was wandering about the Hudson River countryside in search of quiet landscape retreats (Plate 33), sketching picturesque towers that bemused the spectator with glimmering thoughts of remote worlds, or painting delicate patterns of foliage immersed in a golden haze of sentiment. The mood expanded and fed upon itself.

Thomas Cole had in his English boyhood days played the flute and often listened to a Scottish neighbor recounting the border ballads and tales of the wild hills. Later in Ohio, 'his heart was on fire' [42] as he read through an English book on painting technique, lent him by an itinerant German portraitist. It was the final spur to a temperament that longed to lose itself in the poetry of nature. Cole had as a youth worked on engravings for calico prints. He now took to wandering through Ohio and Pennsylvania, sketching rocks and trees, trying to discover the graphic means of 'poetizing' nature.

His dedication to nature became a kind of priesthood, a vigilance over her every mood, her changing lines and hues in all weathers and seasons. These Cole sketched and painted in broad panoramas, searching always for the personal and emotional note. For him, 'whatever scene is chosen, one spirit pervades the whole, light and darkness tremble in the atmosphere and each change transmutes.' In *Dream of Arcadia* (Toledo), *Expulsion from Eden, Oxbow* (Metropolitan), in rainbows, craggy promontories, mountain ranges and torrents, he strove to infuse his own fervor, to humanize and so render them emotionally meaningful.

But in Cole's work this intimate communion between the godhead and man could never be merely implicit. His poetic and religious bent

[42] Louis L. Noble, *Letters and Miscellaneous Papers,* New York, 1853, p. 27.

prompted him to expound his themes in four epic series, including *The Course of Empire* (New York Historical Society) and *The Voyage of Life* (St. Luke's Hospital, New York); his panoramas grew rhetorical and illustrative, formally composed in the manner of Claude and Poussin, but lacking their integration of design. An excess of grandeur and moral sentiment replaced their mystery and sublimity. Only the freshness of the tangled wilderness growth, presented with careful attention to detail, remains significant and distinctly native. A larger element of design and a more intimate delicacy of feeling are observable in Cole's drawings (Plates 42, 46), sketched directly from nature before the moral sentiment is infused.

Cole's moral panoramas were reduced to narrative prose vignettes in the work of Asher B. Durand, who in middle life abandoned his successful career as engraver and turned to portrait and landscape painting. With a graver's eye unused to grappling with broad generalities, Durand restricts his view to the intimate and near at hand; omitting sentiment and moral, he faithfully records the disparate segments of woodland interiors, quiet meadows, and brooks, with delicate precision. If occasionally he achieves a note of fine synthesis, as in *Landscape* (Plate 40) and *Rural Scene* (Plate 44), most often he is fascinated by the texture of gnarled tree trunks (Plate 45), and the fuzz of foliage, the shape and substance of rocky ledges, the glint of sun on stream. His sketchbooks (New-York Historical Society) are a graphic lexicon, prepared with scientific veracity, out of which he composed his literal transcriptions of nature. His eye and hand serve as sure counterparts in a single process that is free from emotional bias, so that his *Thanatopsis, Kindred Spirits,* and *Catskill Dream* retain the bulk content of Romanticism's formal credo without the inner light.

Cole's pupil, Frederick Edwin Church, was a Romanticist turned topographer in color, who replaced the spiritual immanence in nature by the full documentation of pseudo-science. Cole's poesy and Durand's intimacy are broadened to operatic grandeur on canvases of appropriate dimensions. Church wandered from the tropics of South America (Plate 41) to the frozen wastelands of Labrador in search of the marvelous. In his work, tremendous vistas unroll before the astonished eye, nature's outer aspect is recorded with a magnificence and literalness that remind one too easily of railway advertisements and the color-plate illustrations in tourist periodicals. Not nature but her immensity impresses the eye, leaving the sensibilities severely untouched.

Nature had still to wait for a subjective, highly personal rendering that would give it meaning apart from its grandiose or homiletic aspects. Meantime, if photography was rapidly superseding much of portrait painting, these dioramas were to remain unchallenged until the advent of color film. In their own day they were especially welcome in the great mansions of industrial magnates, whose rugged masculinity and limitless enterprise were best reflected in these equally untamed stretches of land. Romanticism had here been stripped of all save the vulgar pursuit of the colossal.

The artists finally retreated from the pioneer's wilderness to civilized and long-cultivated rural regions. It was a retreat marked in part by the melancholy of disillusion. The sweet promise of a redemption of man's nobler self when uncontaminated by urban commercialism and decadent culture had hardly been fulfilled, had turned bitter in actuality. Appropriately enough the glamor of untamed nature had been recorded with metallic precision and calculating eyes; eager to exploit even the sublime in nature, its devotees had embraced the continent and excluded civilization; they had sought out Nature magnificent and forgotten man; at best they were themselves escaping the immediate disillusionment by a retreat to uninhabitable and nonhuman regions. In the end, a reaction against their enumerative realism resulted in an attempt at a personal synthesis of familiar or domesticated landscape achieved through organic composition and tonal harmonies. If often the artist lamely resorted to a blanket suffusion of light to secure a synoptic effect, here and there certain men achieved a broader simplification in handling mass, in the manner of Constable, Wilson, and the Barbizon painters.

The aesthetic shift from the polemics of allegory and the cataloguing of nature's phenomena occurs at last in the work of George Inness, who rapidly absorbed the lexicographic data of Durand and thereupon proceeded to restore the element of subjectivism to landscape. Nature for Inness, an erratic and highly emotional individual, is no longer a matter for factual recording or a setting for a morality; it has become, as in *Home of the Heron* (Chicago) and *Approaching Storm* (Andover), the mirror of his deepest emotional responses and reflections. Exuberant, impetuous, forever experimenting, shifting his point of view, working always at white heat, he made hundreds of quick sketches and instantaneous impressions, searching for the right touch. 'Oh, if I could only catch the subtle mystery of this!'[43] It was not to be done by a treatment of nature 'belittled by trifling detail and puny execution.' Intent on a landscape emotionally expressed and evocative (Plate 66), he found the key to his endeavor in several visits to England and to France especially, where the Barbizon painters, living in close rapport with nature, painted her familiar moods and intimate aspects. In canvases like *Evening at Medford, Massachusetts,* he sought to interpret the crepuscular light on trees that appear as impressionistic silhouettes; on meadows that recede not as countless individual blades of grass but as a broad, suggestive movement of simplified line, mass, and color (Plate 67). And in these interactions of mood between man and nature, Inness pointed the way to a lyrical as opposed to a literal landscape. It was the answer to Cole's puzzled search for the true approach to his theme: the answer of a lyricist, rather than a Romantic in Allston's manner.

The intense search for a method and a meaning in landscape, its moods of melancholy and its solitude, was an inevitable reaction to the Hudson River group's open flattery to the eyes and the patriotic emotions. There followed a gradual withdrawal from an academism of grandeur, to modest views like those of Blakelock, half lost in introspection, a blur of moonlit landscape, a lacework of foliage against a brooding sky.

After a two-week period of instruction, Homer Martin, like Inness, devoted himself to the Hudson River country with a brush always sensitive, almost shy in its sparing use of subject matter. Fascinated by the lonely retreats, he wandered through the countryside, painting its quiet moods of reverie: *Westchester Hills* (Collection of Mrs. Roger Straus);

[43] George Inness, Jr., *Life and Letters of George Inness,* New York, 1917, p. 261.

[20]

Harp of the Winds (New York). Where man had subdued nature and turned to other pursuits, Martin came, seeking her tranquillity, content to brood within her unhurried calm, setting down her multicolored variety with an eye firmly intent on her outer aspects but with a sense of melancholy loneliness that is deepened in these scenes by a furtive play of light.

Man the social and political animal had first been portrayed; then the panoramists depicted the sublime nonhuman backdrop of land towering beyond his reach. Finally, nature was humanized, with man's presence implied. And now, logically, the artist proceeded to restore man himself—in repose, at play, in everyday social activities—within the familiar domesticated landscape. The genre of Inman, Henry Sargent, Woodville, Mount, and others, the comedy of manners of a host of cartoonists and illustrators like Johnston (Plate 51) and Darley (Plate 52), sentimental, caustic, endearing, exposed the young nation in its moments of idleness and buffoonery. Inman studied art in England and returned to paint miniatures, portraits, like that of the poet Halleck, or the brilliant Indian orator, *Red Jacket* (1758-1830) (Plate 37); romantic illustrations (Plate 35); genre, all of them literary, anecdotal, well drawn. In a society growing ever more clamorous and complex, William Sidney Mount devoted himself to the simple and bucolic, a hearty participant in the provincial life of cracker-barrel groups and barnyard activities, setting down with pencil and brush the native idylls of rustic wooing, bargaining tinkers, yarn spinners (Plates 56, 58) with a homespun quality adapted from Brouwer and Jan Steen.

Meanwhile, so rapid was the industrial absorption of the frontier, following hard upon its conquest, that the earlier disillusion almost overnight melted into a nostalgic memory of its faded promise. Large areas were quickly marked off as National Parks to save them from the depradations of lumber and mining interests; reservations were set aside for the Indians. The primitive life had merged into frontier life, and frontier civilization itself was already threatened with urbanization. Much of it was to be recorded by St. Memin (Plate 38), Catlin (Plate 39), Audubon (Plate 47), Bingham (Plates 49, 50, 53, 54), Remington, and that anonymous host of folk artists (Plate 48), many of whom lived with rifle in one hand and pencil in the other.

Samuel Morse had felt that pioneering work, clearing a forest, was no less important than painting. Charles Willson Peale had engaged in politics and art with equal avidity. Caleb Bingham now likewise gave much of his energy to county and state politics, convinced of the prime importance of civic and political participation in the democratic processes by intellectual and creative men. His is the rough-and-tumble frontier life of mid-nineteenth-century America, the free-and-easy, open-river flatboat life on the Missouri and Mississippi, whose denizens are the post-pioneer generation of a semidomesticated but essentially roistering lot of gamblers (Plates 53, 54) and whiskey swillers, the backwash of mushroom-town development.

With a few lessons in painting from the self-taught itinerant Chester Harding, Bingham journeyed to the Pennsylvania Academy, where he copied paintings and lingered over the work of John Neagle. Possessed of a vigorous mind, quick to retort, contemptuous of stupidity, Bingham was at once profoundly receptive to the best traditions in European art, and equally ready to engage in civil affairs, stump speaking, electioneering, soldiering, wading into the critical issues of the day as strenuously as he would examine a rare Old Master abroad, or train his hand at Düsseldorf, or jot down a sketch for one of his canvases of a grizzly codger bent over his hickory cane listening to the election results. With considerable care he composed his studies, working out the design, planning his patterns and color harmonies, combining the austerity of Le Nain with the humor of Steen, but with a home-town quality that is distinctively regional in these scenes of local affairs, town meetings, public-square balloting, stump orating (Plates 49, 50), an exclusively man's world of vested and shirtsleeved interests.

On Native Ground and Foreign

EMERSON'S call to self-reliance and freedom from the encrustations of the past was refreshing to the literary man already supplied with the best of English and German literature and philosophy. In art it carried a connotation full of troubled meaning, a challenge all too true, since there was little European art at hand to study. The trip abroad, generally made in their more mature years, warmed the artists' enthusiasms but had slight effect on styles that had been formed in student days. For them it was pretty much as Homer was to put it: 'If a man wants to be an artist, he should never look at pictures.' But now and then by contrast, a wave of influence from abroad threatened to engulf the artist struggling between native impulse and the brilliant effects emanating from European studios. Succeeding upon the declining influence of British portraiture and neo-classicism, of the landscape work of the Barbizon School and that of Salvatore Rosa, came the schools at Düsseldorf and Munich.

Emanuel Leutze (Plate 57) introduced the vogue for Düsseldorf training, which, under the direction of Schadow, constituted a vigorous two-year preparatory study in 'drawing from the nude, anatomy, perspective and composition' before color work was undertaken. Painting itself was largely a draughtsman's approach, merely substituting color for the line and shading of pencil. With true German regard for infinite detail of documentation, it produced a *trompe l'œil* realism, emphasizing craftsmanship as an end in itself and producing with skill and dexterity living portraits that astonished the eye and carried only their own weight. To a degree it was a salutary influence that reinforced the advice and example of Trumbull and Allston regarding the virtues of draughtsman-

ship, a remedy for the growing practice of bathing structurally defective scenes in an amorphous haze. Actually, the use of color, both to secure plastic value and to contribute to the design of the whole, was little advanced by Düsseldorf training, but its methods were peculiarly apt for the talents of Eastman Johnson.

There is no great psychological penetration or insight in Johnson's portraits. His people live as individuals, as strangers to us; but the attitude, the manner and bearing, the shape of head, the quality of mind that shines through constitute a vital and peculiarly native characterization (Plates 61, 63-5, 86). Almost as a class, America's Rover-boy artists evince an immaturity, a shy unwillingness to probe beyond the endearing features of their reserved sitters, who are not so much individuals as native species and character-symbols. Audubon in his *Delineations of American Scenery and Character* among chapters on The Squatters of the Mississippi, Kentucky Sports, The Original Painter, remarks of the last named: '. . . I should have put him down in my journal for a true Scot. But no:—his tournure, nay the very shape of his visage, pronounced him an American, from the farthest parts of our eastern Atlantic shores.'[44] Johnson's particular merit lies in the nice balance frequently struck between such patriotic sentiment and a certain visual objectivity.

The break from the meticulous formula of the Düsseldorfers was signalized in the retreat from that art center by William Morris Hunt, who was sufficiently Brahmin to take his leave abruptly and wander over to the workshop of Couture in Paris, where he stayed for five years. Hunt had

[44] John J. Audubon, *Delineations of American Scenery and Character* (1837), with an Introduction by F. H. Herrick, New York, 1926, pp. 86-7.

[22]

seen enough of his native soil and read enough of the poetry of Thoreau and Whittier to be drawn to Millet, whom he joined in ardent discipleship and whose work he was among the first to champion and purchase, deriving from it a new notion of the authority of simplicity in great themes.

Hunt's return to America marked the arrival of a force in New England circles, an emanation such as had once drawn a score of artists, from Copley to Morse, to West's studio and the Continent. Quick of perception, full of good talk, sensitive, Hunt brought from Paris something of Whistler's love for sensuous lines and decorative pattern; but more than this, Millet had inculcated in him an awareness of mood and a concern with play of light and tonal values, which he now sought to master in his work.

His own drawing had a grace and refinement often achieved at the expense of solidity. Thus the figure of a boy (Plate 59) in the study for his masterpiece *The Bathers* was quite feminine, but Hunt refused to correct the anatomy for fear of losing the delicate poise of the figure.

To his own students he was at once terrible and inspiring. An endless flow of sharp comment, full of verve, dramatic example, epigrammatic wisdom, literary reference, quotation, stimulated his class to outdo itself. 'To draw! What is it to draw? Any idiot who could learn to write could learn to draw! Not to draw well; for that seems to me to require more skill than anything else in the world.' Or again: 'Don't ask *me! I* don't know how! If I could find out how, I would go ten thousand miles on my knees to do it!' Elsewhere: 'I remember your sketch of a turtle crossing over a garden walk. The most original thing that ever came out of Cambridge.' Suddenly: 'Do! Do! Do! Let it go and do another! You can't finish a thing farther than you can go.' 'When values are so nearly alike that it is difficult to distinguish them, make them alike, and thus learn to simplify your masses.' [45]

Not for Whistler the homespun and folksy, or the gnashing of teeth that Hunt indulged in to frighten local Philistines. An expatriate in the tradition of West and Stuart, Whistler refined on Europe's own refinements. An embattled artist in mortal league against American pragmatism and British academism, Whistler ended by rejecting the materialism of Western art as well, convinced that three dimensionality and the illusionism of perspective were alien to the province of art, whose true concern as manifested in its Oriental origins was with flat, decorative pattern, linear arabesques, and symbolic design. Catholic in his tastes and a dandy in his eclecticism, Whistler roamed the world seeking the methods and materials of his art, turning, as had Lafcadio Hearn, 'Eastern eyes' to seek out the primary decorative patterns of Western life. The result is a thoroughly exotic blossom. His preciosity is less disturbing in some of the drawings and in etchings, like those of the London waterfront life, in which he attempts to balance reality with something akin to Japanese linear grace. Little of Whistler may be called distinctively American beyond his persistent multi-nationalism and a constitutional predilection for revolt.

The cycle of tendencies exhibited in the work of Hunt and Whistler is completed in that of Homer, who rejected all European influence and whose work stands central in the body of graphic expression called American. Homer is almost wholly self-taught, aside from a brief period in a Brooklyn drawing school, some night classes at the National Academy, and a two-year apprenticeship in a lithographer's shop. If America, as Hunt complained, had little more to offer, it is doubtful whether Homer would have sought more. 'I have had no master and never shall have any' comes like Whitman's response to Emerson's call for a new race of poets. In any age Homer would have shied clear of studio palaver or a tasteful eclecticism. His own course was direct, from the rapid, dashing draughtsmanship of Civil War genre themes (Plate 76) done for *Harper's Weekly*, to idyllic images of country life, or to studies of young women caught in the idle moments of their lives (Plate 79), clean-limbed Anglo-Saxons with the turgor of youth silhouetted beneath wind-blown dresses. Occasionally these sketches are structurally vague and verge on the sentimental, but here and there, with a burst of assurance, Homer has seized upon the theme and rendered it masterfully, with an epic breadth of vision and largeness of feeling

[45] William Morris Hunt, *Talks on Art*, edited by Helen M. Knowlton, Boston, 1877, p. 10 *et passim*.

(Plate 75). The approach is wholesome, masculine, forthright, with a touch of boyish immaturity. 'He himself,' writes Lloyd Goodrich, 'was in a sense still a boy who had continued the enjoyments of his country childhood into manhood—fishing, hunting, exploring the countryside—free from the restraints of civilization.' [46]

A trip to England, where Homer visited Tynemouth in Northumberland, directed his attention to the eternal drama of the sea. It marked the limited but intense maturity of the outdoors artist who now turned from the picturesque and idyllic to the somber magnificence of the ever-changing sea and the quiet heroism of men wresting their pleasures and livelihood from her (Plate 78). Like them, Homer is fascinated by her moods, her endless variety, her relentless force and utter splendor. In America's moment of desperate social crisis, a nation embroiled in economic war with herself, Homer steps aside, wanders off to Prout's Neck in Maine to watch the spectacle of a simpler race of men joined against the pitiless forces of nature. And in the end Homer leaves out the men altogether and returns to the native scene as it was before men came, to the vastly older struggle between the slowly yielding shore and the remorseless sea, or the endless wonder of the sea itself, its silent commentary on mortal affairs. There is little of empathy, little of the emotional drag in Homer's sketches, and a consequent lack of integration in his compositions. But a vigorous movement caught by an eye always alert to pattern remains his primary quality, perhaps best revealed in his magnificent water colors.

Scientific Realism

EAKINS' early instruction at the Central High School in Philadelphia, with its exercises in mechanical drawing, perspective, and geometrical forms, was followed by a period of training at the Pennsylvania Academy. Here he followed the traditional methods based on study of the antique, beginning with a long apprenticeship at drawing from casts and copying from paintings, before being permitted to enter the life class in which masked female models occasionally posed. More important, Eakins registered for the anatomy courses at Jefferson Medical College, seriously studying the texts and, along with the class, dissecting cadavers. It was a sincere bid for correctness and thoroughness in fundamental principles. In 1866 he entered the studio of Gérôme in Paris, where he worked vigorously for two years, and then spent several months of concentrated study in Madrid, absorbed in the work of Velasquez and Ribera, impressed, as he wrote home, by their freedom 'from every affectation.' Eakins struggled always against mannerism or style. He was eager for the training at Gérôme's, a method deriving from Ingres' axiom that drawing is the probity of art, and differing only in matters of taste from that at Düsseldorf. Here, too, a painting was merely the systematic, piecemeal coloring of a highly finished drawing, starting at the head and ending at the feet. It was, then, only in Spain that Eakins discovered for himself what 'painting' really was. Back in Philadelphia in 1870, he became professor of drawing and painting at the Academy, with Thomas Anshutz later engaged as his assistant. Eakins now broke with Academy methods and his own training, discarded the antique and the insistence on drawing from casts. Starting his students promptly in oils without preliminary drawing, he taught them to block in their masses and define their structural lines and planes with the brush. It was a revolutionary idea, and at least as old in America as Stuart's method. To Eakins, a protracted period of drawing was a waste of time for the student. 'I think he should learn how to draw with color. . . The main thing that the brush

[46] Whitney Museum, *Winslow Homer Centenary Exhibition*, Introduction by Lloyd Goodrich, 1936, p. 7.

secures is the instant grasp of the grand construction of a figure. There are no lines in nature. . . There are only form and color.' But Eakins, plying both oars, continued to stress drawing as an aid to understanding, rather than as a substructure on which colors were to be overlaid. 'Strain your brain more than your eye,' he urged his students, pressing them to devote much care to the study of perspective, offering a course on it, providing lessons in the use of mechanical-drawing instruments. He invited Dr. William Keen, one of the leading surgeons of the city, to give anatomy lectures as an integral part of the art curriculum, with practice in dissection and drawing for those who had the stomach for it. By 1882 the school was regarded as one of the finest in America. Eakins was elected its director. But his radical methods, his single-minded earnestness, embarrassed some of the trustees and in the end Eakins properly resigned.

If Eakins neglected 'the beauties and graces of painting,' as Isham complained, it was only because those qualities bore no relation to the profounder truth of the period, and in this lies the chief element of his greatness. His are average men and women in a republic, engaged in sports (Plate 87) or intellectual pursuits, surgical operations (Plate 80), games of chess, concerts with the zither or cello. The genre portraiture of Eastman Johnson is here raised by psychological penetration, by maturity of awareness, to great art. For the rest, their difference is the measure of what had taken place in America between the third and last quarters of the nineteenth century. Little wonder that few people cared to sit to Eakins, declining as did Edwin Abbey, 'because he would bring out all the traits of my character that I have been trying to hide from the public for years.' His uncompromising realism, especially in an era when people showed the shock and strain of unmitigated materialism, countenances whipped by competition, could hardly be popular. But the record is there, as surely as that of Copley. It is a record by a great draughtsman, unadorned, scientific, with local overtones that derive from the atmosphere and character of the drab period itself.

Foreign influences persisted, culminating in the single figure of Hunt's pupil, John La Farge, easily the brightest hybrid of European culture, and,

beyond Allston and Hunt, the most richly cultivated and scholarly painter America produced. Though La Farge at the age of six was 'thoroughly drilled in the eighteen-century tradition of drawing by his grandfather' his anatomical draughtsmanship remained weak. His murals (Trinity Church, Boston; Church of the Ascension, New York) and stained-glass designs are the nearest approximation in America to the Renaissance traditions (Plates 72, 73).

Like the return of Allston, Trumbull, and Morse half a century earlier, the arrival of Americans from Munich and Paris after the cessation of civil hostilities was marked by the founding of ateliers and the organizing of exhibitions that now approached the stature and bore the cosmopolitan air of the foremost European studios.

Eakins' own direct approach to painting was already in great vogue through the studies of Duveneck (Plate 89), Chase (Plate 92), and Shirlaw (Plate 96), of the Munich School. The niggling draughtsmanship of the Düsseldorf School had been abandoned at Munich in favor of working directly with heavily loaded brush on canvas, painting in constructional planes, disposing masses directly with abrupt vigorous brushstrokes. It was an astonished and excited Boston in 1875 that gazed at the everyday native faces looming out of impenetrable Rembrandtesque backgrounds. The bravura effects achieved with an air of studied casualness, the flat patchwork of planes and color harmonies done with what appeared to be brilliant technical virtuosity, caught the popular imagination and persuaded it that America was really producing Old Masters. At any rate, the Munich technique did carry, in its rapid brushstroke and palpable textual tonalities, clear-cut elements of impressionism that reappeared in Manet as something profounder than virtuosity, as the essence of reality born in light, and this in turn was reinterpreted by Robert Henri as a simple impressionism of personal response to the familiar, vibrantly mirrored as a segment of the living scene.

Parisian Impressionism superseded Düsseldorf and Munich, playing for quick, blurred images of color areas, the impact of light on surface texture; modeling by contrast of color plane rather than line—'There are no lines in nature'—and catching the glitter of outdoor sunlight by juxtaposing complimentary spots of pure pigment. American Impressionists rendered their versions with considerable originality: John Twachtman (Plate 101), working always with great delicacy; Maurice Prendergast (Plate 103), absorbed in his color mosaics; J. Alden Weir (Plate 93), intent on nuances of light and tonal harmonies; Childe Hassam (Plate 95), with an eye always to gay splashes of color; Mary Cassatt (Plate 94), with brush sensitive to attitudes of grace. Equally important, these artists worked for the same rhythmic effects, studied the same play of light, whether in color or simple black and white. At the very moment when the influence from abroad threatened by its seductive prettiness and coloristic brilliance to overwhelm them, they held out for the virtues of draughtsmanship characterized by acute sensitiveness and a Japanese delicacy of line. And in the very act of leaving their studios to take their *plein-air* themes wherever the play of light fell, they were joined with considerable eagerness by a group of young artists who had also turned their attention to the everyday drama that was being enacted outside studio doors. Though for them it was not so much nature as it was man in his native setting that played the principal role.

The Realism of the Newspaper School

IN the decade following the end of the War between the States, civil reform attempted to grapple with political corruption, while the graphic arts reported the battle in progress. The 1870's, which saw the full flowering of Tammany Hall and the Tweed Ring, witnessed also the triumph of Thomas Nast, who excoriated Boss Tweed and his cohorts in a series of cartoons for *Harper's Weekly*. Honoré Daumier in France had been thrown into jail for his impudence in caricaturing the chiefs of state. Tammany could only resort to bribery: Nast was offered half a million dollars to go abroad and 'study art.' His retort was a cartoon in *Harper's* that had the snarling Tiger lashing her tail, or else (as in Plate 84) trounced on her back for the moment.

If Nast's fame rests largely on these indictments of a corrupt municipal administration, his significance as a draughtsman derives from his taciturn calligraphic wit and his linear intensity. He abandoned the old, elaborate cartoon, heavily freighted with allegorical meaning, crowded in detail, and created a style that concentrated on a single dramatic point, never subtle but explosive.

In addition to *Harper's,* the other weeklies ran cartoons and sketches that filled their pages with lively comment on the social scene. But it was only when the daily press began to utilize the artist's work extensively that the graphic idiom really took on native vigor and character. Two kinds of artists were employed: the cartoonist and the sketch artist. The former, whose cartoon, conceived and drawn at short notice under pressure, turned directly to the symbol, to the swift summing-up of a political situation with a 'visual figure of speech,' developed as a result 'a graphic shorthand, a deft simple statement of the issue, economical in line and emphatic in its effect.' This applied to the sketch artist as well. The *Daily Graphic,* the first illustrated daily in America, assigned Kemble, Frost, C. J. Taylor (Plate 100), and W. A. Rogers to depict familiar scenes and daily events. But it was not until the invention of the Linotype in 1886, which more than tripled the number of daily newspapers, that the work of the sketch artist became a regular and necessary feature of the daily press. With the half-tone process as yet unknown, newspapers had to rely on staff artists for illustrations of human-interest stories and on-the-spot sketches of personalities and events of the moment. The introduction of feature stories in the evening newspapers and especially in the Sunday editions, which mushroomed in the last two decades of the century, called for even more drawings.

By far the most interesting artists and free-lance illustrators were those of the Philadelphia group: William Glackens, John Sloan, George Luks, and Everett Shinn, all trained at the Pennsylvania Academy, then the liveliest center of art instruction in the country. They had been steered away from the popular academic-romantic approach by several factors: the energetic counsel of their teacher Thomas Anschutz, who as former student and colleague of Eakins preached the new realism in art; the growing naturalistic trend in American literature; the tide of nineteenth-century liberal thought that reached American shores in the philosophy of Marx and hurled its strength against the bulwarks of a complacent society; and finally, the fact that as sketch artists of a great daily, expected to tell the many-sided story of a teeming city, they became steeped in the imagery of everyday life.

The guiding spirit of the newspaper group was Robert Henri, who had come to Philadelphia to study under Anschutz and formed there the life-long association with his colleagues that was to have important consequences for the development of their art. When he returned from an extended stay in Europe, he brought with him the gospel of the masters who had chosen to paint the humble as well as the great, who had celebrated life wherever they had found it—Rembrandt, Velasquez, Goya, Manet. Henri himself drew with the same dash and vigor that distinguished his painting. His sketch of a boatman (Plate 107) lacks the linear precision of Luks, but the memory-image of burly features, truculent expression, brawn and muscle, is here seized by means of impressionistic, slashing strokes. For him the rising tempo of life ruled out all academism:

Oh! the long and dreary years of learning to draw! How can a student after the drudgery of it look at a man or an antique statue with any other emotion than a plumb-bob estimate of how many lengths he has. . . What you must express in your drawing is not 'what model you had' but 'what were your sensations.' [47]

Henri's insistence on the quick sketch had come as it were in the nick of time. The year 1900 saw him established in New York, where he taught at

[47] Robert Henri, *The Art Spirit*, compiled by Margery Ryerson, Philadelphia, 1923, p. 75.

the Chase School. Everett Shinn had also moved in, and soon the other members of the Newspaper School followed. They continued to turn out, in addition to their canvases, quantities of drawings for the New York papers and magazines, working with an eye for the anecdotal, observed with humor and sympathy, recorded with warmth and wit. The academies were now abandoned for the city streets, and this early training was to show its strength in the work of the mature painters.

John Sloan, sketching for the *Masses, Collier's,* and *Harper's,* did some of his best work during this period. His memorable series of cartoons for the *Masses,* which he helped to edit, did much to establish its brilliant reputation. The roster of men who worked for the socialist weekly during its brief existence has since grown august with hall-of-fame respectability. Henri contributed, among other things, a superb satirical drawing, *Judging Art,* in which he lampooned the jury, his pet aversion; undistinguished draughtsman but hard-hitting political cartoonist, Art Young hammered out social criticism, as did Robert Minor and Maurice Becker; Stuart Davis' drawing in the flat poster style (preceding his abstract phase) lent a decorative though often incongruous touch to pages carrying Max Eastman's earnest exhortations; Abraham Walkowitz perpetuated in delicate, flowing lines the fleeting grace of Isadora Duncan; Albert Sterner, upon whom Cortissoz bestowed the ultimate praise that he 'drew like a gentleman,' provided a touch of the grand manner; Maurice Sterne's expert draughtsmanship ranged from sensual plasticity to semi-abstract linear composition; Jo Davidson's pen traced graceful, airy studies of dancing figures; Arthur B. Davis, Glenn O. Coleman, Eugene Higgins, Glackens, Bellows, Mahonri Young—all worked in techniques that differed as widely as their subject matter, all of them prodigal with ideas, with talents quickened by the unprecedented interest of an eager public.

Sloan's drawings for the *Masses* deal largely with the themes of social injustice. His searching pencil exposed the sanctimony of the Women's Night Court, the myth of race superiority, or, in what is perhaps his most powerful drawing, *State Police in Philadelphia* (Plate 111), the strong-arm methods employed to terrorize organized labor. Sloan was always the news reporter, objectively observing, conscientiously recording. As artist, he sought to transform facts into aesthetic experience, and in rare instances his work, for sheer linear virtuosity and symbolic imagery, is hardly inferior to that of Delacroix and Daumier. By 1914, he had gained complete mastery of every black-and-white medium and had learned to draw with directness and veracity, instantly communicating his thought.

Most prolific and ablest draughtsman in the newspaper group was William J. Glackens. 'Throughout his distinguished career,' says Shinn, 'Glackens made thousand of drawings. At the end of a working day his studio floor was literally covered with them. These were done with lightning speed and repeated many times, until he had become so familiar with his subject that he could place them in his picture without even referring to the sketches.'[48] A genial and sympathetic observer of the life around him (Plates 106, 108), Glackens was a constant inspiration to the others who worked with him. All paid tribute to his unflagging interest, which often revived their own drooping spirits, to his photographic memory, and, above all, to his extraordinary facility with the pencil. By storing up salient details in his memory and merely jotting down a few rapid notes, a stroke here and there, he was able, back at his drawing board, to reproduce an incredible variety of facial expressions, gestures, and attitudes, whether of a tense group of spectators or a swarm of children with their parents and nurses in the park. His pen 'bored with uncanny precision into the very soul of all his characters. It pronged them on its point and whirled them into life. Like a hypodermic needle, the black fluid probed and filled the veins, built bones and clothed his people, motivating them and giving them purpose.'[49]

George Luks also served his apprenticeship on the daily press. As war correspondent and sketch artist for the *Philadelphia Bulletin,* he observed and recorded the Cuban Rebellion of 1895-6; later he joined the group of illustrators on the *Philadelphia Press,* and when the *New York World* began to print its first colored Sunday comics, Luks succeeded Outcault, the creator of the 'Yellow Kid' comic strip. Originally based on European models,

the comic strips, having become the most popular feature of the Sunday supplements, soon developed native character and humor. In a sense they were the forerunners of the movies, evincing that dynamic element for which the fast-growing, fast-moving American public showed so marked a preference. Even the liveliest cartoon now seemed static compared with the comic strip, which provided for its characters a never-ending series of adventures and perplexities, told in graphic metaphors unmistakably homemade.

Having spent his early childhood as a breaker boy in the coal mines of Pennsylvania, Luks was naturally drawn to the teeming masses who furnished the 'copy' for his early drawings. 'I like to draw the man in the street,' he told his friends, 'the woman in the train, the children in the park—or in the gutter, as it happens. I want a chance to see and observe and think deeply about the person I'm going to sketch. I want to understand where he belongs or where chance has put him.' In his *Studies of Men's Heads* (Plate 105) one senses the affectionate sympathy for people that is at the basis of Luks' work. A student of Hals' slashing brushstroke, Luks was above mere virtuosity in painting; his drawings are the careful studies of a researcher determined to understand the nature of his subject matter (Plate 109). 'I have learned that you can't do the real thing from the outside in,' he said. 'You've got to know the mind to draw the man.'[50]

Everett Shinn, the fourth member of the Philadelphia group, worked as sketch artist for the *Enquirer* and then for the *Philadelphia Press.* Like a cub reporter, he was dispatched to cover murders, trials, fires, prize-fights, and coal-mine disasters. He had a facile way of drawing, and his early work is much closer in spirit to the realistic newspaper idiom of Luks and Glackens than was the early poster style of Sloan. But as Shinn matured, the ease and virtuosity with which he drew proved a pitfall; his line lost much of its incisiveness and elegance and came near being slick and superficial. The early New York sketches (1900-1905) caught the feel of the city with precision and nervous intensity; whether he was communicating his ideas

[48] Everett Shinn, 'William Glackens as an Illustrator,' *The American Artist,* 1945, p. 22.
[49] Ibid.

[50] Mary Fanton Roberts, 'Painting Real People—Is the Purpose of George Luks' Art,' *Touchstone Magazine,* vol. VIII, Oct. 1920, pp. 32-8.

of east-side streets, or Chinatown (Plate 115), or fashionable matinee crowds, there was nothing contrived or mechanical in his statements. Curious contrast is offered, however, by the dazzling illustrations, devoid of meaning, that he did throughout the 'twenties and 'thirties for the *Metropolitan Magazine,* and by the pastel studies of dancers, which echo the grace of Degas without that master's tonic ugliness and vehement distortions.

The syndicated features introduced by Hearst, Scripps, and other newspaper chains did away with the insatiable demand for newspaper illustration, for one artist could now do the work of fifty. Moreover, the half-tone process, now in wide use, no longer depended on line drawings since it could reproduce photographs equally well. Newspaper sketches that illustrated events of the day became a thing of the past, so that after 1914 editors rarely assigned an artist to cover a news story. A superb artistic medium had been given vigorous life by one scientific invention, the Linotype, and its scope greatly curtailed by another—the half-tone process. Although magazines of distinction continued to use drawings by contemporary artists, newspaper illustration as an art was not again revived. In later decades, artists like Boardman Robinson and William Gropper were to contribute brilliant graphic commentary to the press, but these drawings were special features rather than everyday reportage.

The newspaper artists had made a notable contribution not only by raising the level of journalistic illustration but, more important, by observation and rendition of the everyday scene through full participation in the march of events around them. They chose the picturesque, the pathetic, or the charming aspects of American life, not for the sake of any of these qualities, but took 'life as it was—the squalor of overcrowded city slums, the merriment of children at play, the bustle and confusion of crowds—and sought to impart the significance they found in it. Thus it was given to them to record the essential character of the America of their day.'

America was no stranger to realism, but was unprepared for the reportorial vehemence that the newspaper men introduced. Paintings such as *Scrubwomen in the Library, Hester Street, New York, The Bread Woman,* gave an unflinching account of certain phases of city life neglected by the Academy winners. There was little of the academician in Glackens. Even his book illustrations were alarmingly suggestive of life in the raw, or uncomfortably satiric. Nor was Luks academic timber. His scores of drawings of 'the saloons and drinking places—*The Bucket of Blood, Paddy the Pig's* . . . men being thrown out, drunks spilling in their cups, pell mell, bodies on the floor or piled up under the table,' [51] were not likely to bring him into favor with society's more respectable members.

Not directly associated with the Newspaper School, but also treating scenes of contemporary life with social sympathy, were a number of Henri's students and several others who communicated their thoughts expressively in graphic form: George Overbury ('Pop') Hart, George Bellows, Glenn O. Coleman, Boardman Robinson, Mahonri Young, and Eugene Higgins. A picaresque figure in American art, 'Pop' Hart roamed over several continents in his search for the vivid and exuberant aspects of life. He filled his sketchbooks with calligraphic exclamations of joy, gusto, and sly humor at the life around him, whether in Europe, Africa, the South Seas, or in his native America. Combining several mediums in his drawing technique, Hart often established the general background by means of broad washes or smudges of charcoal, across which his pen moved finely, accenting features and expressions (Plate 116). At the other extreme from studio drawings, these random sketches of men at their tasks and pleasures sound a note of gaiety mounting to exhilaration.

An accomplished lithographer and essentially a draughtsman, George Bellows was perhaps the most enthusiastic exponent of the graphic media among the artists of his generation. Critics have spoken of his 'sense of the sufficiency of black and white.' He was, indeed, at his best when working in the draughtsman's medium, exploited subtly and dramatically. Only rarely do his paintings convey that sense of complete harmony of theme related to treatment that is invariably present in his hundreds of drawings and lithographs. His realism, like that of the early Flemish masters, hovers between intimacy and detachment,

[51] Jerome Mellquist, *The Emergence of an American Art,* New York, 1942.

revels in lustiness tempered by sobriety, resting on a deep satisfaction in material well-being offset by a constant seeking for spiritual values.

If it is true that American art is pre-eminently an expression of middle-class spirit, then Bellows is its spokesman *par excellence*. The portrait studies of the members of his family are, for the most part, devoid of psychological insight, revealing merely a fondness and indulgence born of constant and satisfying contact (Plate 121). Intensely American, too, is Bellows' sense of justice, deeply roused in such a drawing as *The Law is Too Slow*, a furious indictment of lynching, and his constant preoccupation with action involving opposition and conflict. Most often this conflict is expressed not overtly but by means of spatial relationships—a mathematic of the emotions; and this dynamism too is part of his American heritage (Plate 114).

Bellows was one of the contributors to the *Masses* in the days when that periodical was reproducing the work of the ablest draughtsmen in the country. He was primarily interested in defining values by means of line, juxtaposing black-and-white masses to create dynamic form. He said:

Subject matter is motivation; pattern is plot, drawing is *performance*. Whether the instrument is pen or crayon or brush-with-oil color, the moment it moves upon the picture, drawing is coming into existence; we who look at the picture deduce the subject matter and apprehend the pattern, but the performance we re-enact.[52]

Glenn O. Coleman, another of the 'Pre-War Realists,' studied with Henri and Shinn. Ohio-born, he came to New York shortly after 1900. The many-faceted life of the metropolis, especially its teeming east side (Plate 104) and Greenwich Village, fired his imagination. In a series of drawings, lithographs, and paintings, sometimes purely descriptive, sometimes moody and full of overtones, he told the story of the city he loved and sought to express. Most of Coleman's works were bought by fellow artists who relished his highly individual accounts of the places they frequented—the burlesques, the Bowery, Chinatown, Coney Island, the Atlantic, and the Haymarket. Now and then Coleman would abandon his role of troubadour of the

city streets and, in a *New Masses* drawing, such as *Jefferson Market Jail* and *A Great Joke*, take issue sharply with a system that created grotesquely tragic incongruities. Like his fellow artist and biographer, Stuart Davis, Coleman abandoned, under the influence of the Ecole de Paris, his early realistic manner for abstract treatment.

The realism of Sloan, Bellows, and Coleman tapers off into a gently realistic mannerism in the work of Jerome Myers. A Southerner who made his home in New York, Myers in his drawings of ghetto slums, breadlines, mission tents, children in tattered clothes playing along the waterfront, tired men and women asleep on the recreation piers in the paralyzing heat of a New York summer, chose to ignore the squalor, tedium, and banality of life among the poor for pathos, humor, and quaintness. A prolific and facile draughtsman, he made hundreds of wistful vignettes, rich in detail, modest and sensitive in line.

Living in the slums of New York had a very different effect on Boardman Robinson. Neither the physical nor the moral ugliness of this submerged environment was lost on him. He understood all its grim and sordid implications. When in 1906 he accepted a job with the Association for Improvement of the Condition of the Poor, he himself was penniless; and wandering with sketchbook in hand through the sunless, congested streets of the east side, he noted down the stories of tragedy and frustrations written in the faces of the poor. For him there was no escape either into pathos or fantasy. Art did not stop with the telling of a story. Something of man's hope and struggle always contrived to turn the tale into a prayer, a warning, a stern denunciation.

When the *Morning Telegraph* assigned him to cover the theatre and night life about New York, he was able to make the most of his gift for social satire and wit; stage folk seldom minded being caricatured as long as it kept them in the public eye. Robinson did as many as twenty drawings each week, candid and caustic quips, in a slashing, telling line. By 1914 his cartoons were appearing in *Puck* and *Harper's* along with those of Henri, Sloan, Luks, and Bellows. The turning point of Robinson's career came the following year when, with John Reed, he undertook to cover the Eastern Front for the *Metropolitan Magazine*. The Balkans

[52] George Bellows, Foreword, *The Paintings of George Bellows*, New York, 1929, pp. viii-xi.

were a hazardous assignment. Together they caught the horror that swept over onetime peaceful valleys and industrious lands, and observed the agony of uprooted refugees and shattered homes. They saw and noted down—John Reed in his rich, personal style and 'Mike' Robinson in his swift, concentrated line—the impact of war on people of the most opposite and various kinds, of manifold racial strains, and different religions and nationalities (Plates 125, 126). The illustrated articles they sent back to the *Metropolitan* were prototypes for the best traditions in foreign correspondence, equaling in graphic power the finest latter-day reportage.

When he returned from his trip to the Balkans and Russia, Robinson aligned himself with the left-wing writers and artists, particularly the group active in the *Masses*, and after its suppression in 1917, the *Liberator*, for which he did some of his most effective cartoons (*Putting Democracy at Home under Lock and Key; Russia Surrounded,* etc.). His mature style is rich and varied; with pen and ink he is capable of bold patterns, complex relations of form, subtle suggestions of mood and character. His figures evoke the monumentality of Michel Angelo and something of that master's brooding sense of tragedy (Plate 131). While his cartoons continued to supply savage comment on the current political scene, Robinson illustrated a number of books, notably several Russian classics, as well as *Moby Dick* and *Spoon River Anthology*. Here, too, he is the passionate participant rather than the onlooker, not content with decorative description or faithful narration, but always intent on penetrating the emotional recesses of the mind, laying bare the violent and tortuous passages of the human psyche. It is an art welded on the forge of realism, tempered in the heat of political partisanship.

Despite its grace and delicacy, there is something stark and primitive about the art of Mahonri Young, grandson of the famous Brigham. Stretches of shadowless desert across which gaunt, primeval plant forms march in geometric procession; trees whose branches weave an ever changing pattern; taut, muscular men at work, bodies flexed for effort; the movements of wild animals—the vigor inherent in these themes Mahonri Young stated with honesty and firmness of line. He possessed none of the reformer's zeal; he studied men at their labors because the tension and drama of the human body pitting its strength against material resistance afforded him aesthetic satisfaction. 'My love for work and the worker is not sociological at all,' he once explained. 'It is a sheer response to an art impulse. I like what workers do; I like their poise and balance.'[53] If his bronzes with their broad modeling are fully realized, their multiplied planes flowing into each other, as Mather observes, 'insensibly, without any rough clay passages,' his drawings, defining the human figure broadly and massively, are no less convincing. His lines are at once plastic and impressionistic, audacious and essentially calligraphic, as in *The Shovellers* (Plate 112). The sweat is here distilled or sublimated in laws of line and motion. Lloyd Goodrich draws attention to Young's 'continual search for the quality of line which will give the greatest sensation of form and movement' (Plate 160). It is this quality, inherent in his studies of human beings, that lends them always a feeling of pent-up vitality.

Unlike Young, Eugene Higgins turned to the proletariat for entirely sociological reasons. True, it was under the overwhelming influence of Daumier and Millet that Higgins, as a young student in Paris, drew for the socialist paper *Assiette de Beurre*: somber figures of 'the very poor, skulking through the little dark squares at Montmartre, the criminal making deep shadows against the grey walls of old fortifications, children crouching away from dark outlines known as fathers; women uncouth and shapeless, enticing lovers along the quays . . .' But his brooding over the poor is also part of his American inheritance—compassion for the dispossessed, a democratic conviction that happiness is an inalienable right. The son of a stonecutter, Higgins never quite escaped the memory of stubborn wrestling with granite, for many of his compositions retain the feeling of form wrenched out of chaos. Building up his drawings by means of broad washes, he likes to outline his figures in heavy contours, effecting a strong chiaroscuro scheme that potently conveys an elegiac mood (Plate 117).

[53] Mary Fanton Roberts, 'An Art Born in the West and Epitomizing the West: Illustrated from the Work of Mahonri Young,' *Touchstone Magazine*, vol. IV, 1918, pp. 8-18.

Pioneers of American Modernism

MEN like Sloan, who had avoided direct contact with Europe, nevertheless accepted the spirit of inquiry that for more than half a century sustained French art and kept it vigorously flourishing. By the time these influences directly reached our shores, they had been so well anticipated that they barely shocked even the academicians; it was not until the famous Armory Show flung Post-Impressionism into the teeth of conservative New York art circles that the impact of the new movement shattered the comparative isolationism of our art. While critics denounced, academicians reviled, and the public flocked to see the freakish contortions, Cézanne, Matisse, and Picasso came to stay.

Henri and his followers, who had joined in sponsoring the Armory Show, helped to bring about a strong reaction against their own once-revolutionary realism. For Post-Impressionism, which in Europe had swung away from academic naturalism and the last, scientific phase of Impressionism, made its strongest appeal in America to a group of younger men who, surfeited with the 'human interest' art of the Eight, had turned to the Ecole de Paris, which emphasized simplification of form, stylistic experiments in many directions, notably cubistic analysis and abstraction—the accent being always on self-expression, creating rather than recording. It was a curious, impersonal lyricism, often exaggerating, distorting. In varying measure, the theories and techniques current in Europe attracted two generations of artists, among them Walt Kuhn, once a cartoonist drawing delightful 'funnies,' organizer and prime mover of the Armory Show, whose dependence upon Matisse and Picasso is evident in *Woman Clown* (Plate 119), in which simplicity of line is carried to the height of dramatic expression; Henry Lee McFee, whose natural tendency to isolate and simplify forms

became intensified as a result of his studies in Cubism, *The City* (Plate 127) being concerned mainly with the relationship of planes in space, delicately yet firmly stated; Charles Demuth, whose illustrations for the tales of Henry James and Edgar Allan Poe owe much, in their introspection and reticence, to the work of the *Fauves*. Most of Demuth's work is done in colored washes over which a sensitive line weaves back and forth, telling its story with grace and irony. John Marin, Joseph Stella, and Alfred Maurer were among the *avant-garde* who helped to widen the gap between the intellectual modernists and the American realists, as was William Zorach, one of the earliest students of Cubism, who, some twenty years before he turned to sculpture, was deeply interested in 'the organization of planes in a continuous rhythmic pattern,' evident in his expressive drawings (Plate 153), as in his later direct-cut plastic works.

Almost a decade before the Armory Show, Max Weber was discovering in the Paris studio of his teacher, Henri Matisse, that modern art could study the older civilization to its advantage. He explored the painting and sculpture of the ancient Orient—Assyria, Egypt, Persia, archaic Greece, and Sung China—the fruits of his avid research earning him the title of eclectic. A deeply personal emotionalism counteracted this assimilative tendency and saved him from carrying on mere intellectual experiment in cross-fertilization. His *Head of a Woman* (Plate 124), restrained as a Sung painting, suggests in place of Chinese aloofness a mood of elegy and monumentality.

Alfred Stieglitz, who in his famous Photo-Secession Gallery at 291 Fifth Avenue displayed the first canvases by Cézanne, Matisse, and Picasso to be shown in this country, also sponsored the work of younger Americans: Georgia O'Keeffe, who

[32]

became his wife; Kuhn and Demuth, Marin, Stella, Dove, Maurer, Zorach, Weber, Walkowitz, Hartley, and Sheeler. Abraham Walkowitz struck a variety of chords and discords before he attained compositional mastery. Intuitively he grasped the search of the *Fauves* for expressive pattern and rhythm. Hundreds of his drawings show an increasing facility in solving the problem of fluidity and motion in linear form, while certain of his studies, like *Man of Iron* (Plate 129), convey a corresponding sense of solidity and repose.

Charles Sheeler, born in Philadelphia, trained at the Pennsylvania Academy, early found his way to Europe and the Ecole de Paris, where experiments in structure analysis engaged his interest. Isolating his forms, he stripped them of nonessentials, so that their true nature could be set forth with logic and lucidity. Experimenting with both cubist and abstract art, he was strict in his avoidance of the emotional and editorial in his attempt to remove, as he put it, 'the method of painting as far as possible from being an obstacle in the way of consideration of the picture.' In defense of photographic realism, he asserts: 'My interest in photography has been based on admiration for its possibility of accounting for the visual world with an exactitude not equaled by any other medium.' His meticulous method, more pronounced in his highly finished drawings (Plate 151) than in his paintings, where color modifies unequivocal delineation, devotes itself to industrial and provincial Americana: the Ford plant at Dearborn; the white barns of Bucks County, Pennsylvania; the bare and beautiful interior of a Shaker kitchen.

The very antithesis of Sheeler's painstaking realism is to be found in the work of Marsden Hartley, poet-painter whose technique was fashioned in Europe while his vision remained rooted in America. An early Expressionist, spiritual kin of Ryder, he learned from the *Fauves* and later the German Expressionists to create mood and emotion by means of color and line which, as with Matisse and Derain, 'sang their freedom from descriptive drudgery.' Hartley has drawn and painted Mount Katahdin in Maine with the devotion of Cézanne's vigil over the ever changing aspects of Mont Ste. Victoire. In his drawings especially one feels the artist reaching out for the most direct and personal, the least formally descriptive approach to the austere beauty of the north country (Plate 122).

Abstraction and simplification are the keynotes of Georgia O'Keeffe's flawless art, which re-creates nature forms at their most elemental, yet full of rich and unsuspected beauty. Although her locale is American, the gnarled trees, bleached bones, desert plants, and autumn leaves which she transcribes with such sparing yet dramatic means are fixed neither in time nor place, belonging rather to some universal reservoir of art forms. She draws with complete mastery of technique, holding her objects up to graphic scrutiny with a clairvoyance even more impressive when she works in black and white.

Maturing somewhat later than this first group of abstractionists were Preston Dickinson, who also turned from literal representation to form analysis, achieving solidity of design and often an Oriental richness of pattern, particularly in his graphic work (Plate 132), and Morris Kantor, stylistically related to the *Fauves* but fond of introducing psychological and literary overtones into his work. Ernest Fiene has shown a strong interest in formal relations without abandoning the traditional, descriptive element, which is present in fresh, lyric mood in his New England landscapes. Jules Pascin, American by adoption, belongs temperamentally and stylistically to France, but his influence on some of our contemporary artists, notably Adolf Dehn, George Biddle, and Emil Ganso, has been considerable. His draughtsmanship is expert and resourceful; his pen satiric, biting, often gay and frolicsome.

Regional and Social Commentators

AS the period preceding the First World War saw the Henri group reflecting in art the interests of Crane and Dreiser in literature, so the writing of the 'twenties, documentary, analytical, naturalistic—the reportage of Sinclair Lewis, Elmer Rice, Hemingway, and Wolfe—was paralleled by the work of Henri's students and followers—Edward Hopper, Eugene Speicher, Guy Pène du Bois, Alexander Brook. Where literature assayed the whole complex of socio-pathological analysis and the attendant impulse to escape, art likewise began to concern itself with psychological values, to articulate its thoughts in a less literal, more introspective manner. Thus realism became implicit rather than explicit in Kuniyoshi and Watkins, and assumed a dreamlike quality in the bright images of Francis Criss and Peter Blume.

Edward Hopper and Eugene Speicher are wholly factual in their rendering of the American and his habitat. The Armory Show, while vindicating the preference of their colleagues for stylistic experiment, left Hopper and Speicher unperturbed, content to pursue their examination of the familiar scene, noting with ever increasing nostalgia details that once had passed unnoticed or been taken for granted. Neither the new vision, which in 1913 burst upon their sight, nor the stimulating experience of study abroad was strong enough to dislodge these men from their position as sober, factual recorders of the homely scene. Hopper's firm grasp in handling formal relations, his dramatic massing of dark and light areas, whether in his wind-swept lighthouses, deserted streets, ramshackle urban dwellings, or the silhouetting of *Manhattan Bridge* (Plate 118), achieve a sense of solidity and force. Speicher's drawings of nudes, as well as his portraits, demonstrate 'a resolute and deliberate taking possession of the form in a monumental aspect,'

strikingly exemplified in his studies of *Red Moore, the blacksmith* (Plate 143).

Guy Pène du Bois has for many years been exposing the snobbishness and sham aestheticism of the upper social levels. He has pitted his art against the smugness, the dowager respectability, the potbellied benevolence of the suburban and urban milieu. Like Sinclair Lewis, he has questioned values and attacked standards, but his ample brokers, full-bosomed matrons, and simpering hostesses are too often straw figures, set up for the effective thud of their moral collapse. When it is not too obviously a satire of manners, his account of the contemporary scene is richly revealing (Plate 113). Solidly modeling in warm colors or plastically handled lines, he builds his composition on a sound, three-dimensional framework, achieving the firmness of contour and integrality of Renoir's classical period.

Du Bois' contempt for the banality of middle-class America is altogether absent in the regionalism of Thomas Benton (Plate 139), John Steuart Curry (Plate 142), Grant Wood (Plate 138), and Charles Burchfield, which is at once a development of earlier realism and a reaction against the sweeping international movement in art. The most vociferous protagonist of the midwestern regionalists, Benton has singled out picturesque and obvious Americana for his subject matter, delineating his hillbillies, Ozark scenes, and folklore characters with an aggressive, flamboyant line which, despite his frequent denunciations of everything alien to American realism, owes as much to the Italian Baroque as it does to German Expressionism. Pursuing his studies on the Continent, Grant Wood found the earliest German masters much to his liking: their homely charm, their tidiness, their exact and glowing realism. It was in this spirit of fidelity and intimacy that he rendered his account of Iowa's folkways.

Challenged by a decade of economic depression and political chaos to find a formula expressive of altered circumstance and vision, some of our artists translated into their work the tension and strife of social forces, while neo-romantics like Eugene Berman and Tchelichev turned nostalgically to the past, reassembling scattered fragments of an older aesthetic pattern to clothe the raw and unsightly present. Still others, Peter Blume (Plate 158), Francis Criss, and Julio de Diego among them, explored Surrealism in their attempt to create a reality dependent not upon literal realism but a personal architecture of ideas and symbols, subjectively related.

Social awareness, which had quickened with the Civil War in Spain, with the growing recognition of the Fascist menace, and with the bitter lack of employment at home, became the inspiriting element in the work of William Gropper. A boyhood spent on New York's lower east side, an artistic-social credo shaped by the counsel of Henri and Bellows, a natural gift for terse, epigrammatic comment, and a knowledge of the ills that weaken the social organism—on these four cornerstones Gropper built his structure. It was inevitable that his social sympathy should express itself in political cartoons. Like many of his older colleagues, he drew for the newspapers; much of his best work was done for left-wing periodicals, to which he contributed throughout the 'thirties. A trip to Soviet Russia, which he took in the company of Sinclair Lewis and Theodore Dreiser, resulted in a series of drawings so vivid and dramatic that they at once placed him in the front ranks as a draughtsman. Massing his black-and-white areas with the intensity of a Goya, he projects his ideas in lines now bold and flowing, now broken, angular, and sharply exclamatory. Far from being constantly at odds with the world,

Gropper takes a lusty delight in man's work and his pleasures, yielding to an irrepressible exuberance of line (Plate 161).

The critical appraisal of society, which forms the core of Gropper's work and motivates that of Mitchell Siporin (Plate 155), Jack Levine, Louis Ribak, George Biddle, Aaron Sopher, Joseph Hirsch, and others, is not confined to those generally grouped among the realists. Men like Philip Evergood, Anton Refregier, Louis Guglielmi, and Robert Gwathmey, rephrasing the language of realism by juxtaposing images not visibly related, have voiced the same criticism and sympathy. Surrealism has been used with striking effect by these men to suggest the disintegration and nameless terror that haunt the disjointed world today. The achievement of these artists is usually measured by their canvases and murals, but their drawings reveal far more of their personal vision than their studied and formal designs.

The feverish and multifaceted activity of the war years has not been without effect on the contemporary artist. In every corner of the land and in the most unexpected byways of the social scene, a proliferation of drawings has marked the work of Reginald Marsh, Louis Bouché, Aaron Bohrod, Adolf Dehn, Peggy Bacon, Wanda Gag, Francis Chapin, Harry Wickey, Paul Cadmus, the Soyers, and a host of others. Concerned with men and manners, with Coney Island sideshows, burlesques, barbershop interiors, Georgia crackers, cocktail parties, Minnesota kitchens, Chicago slums, baseball, New York office girls, and prairie sunsets, with the personal vision, the slap of satire, the lyric memento, few things appear to escape the draughtsman's notice. Invariably he is concerned with the detailed, idiosyncratic, specific documentation of his theme, not always superbly realized, but recorded with extraordinary zest and often a fine eye and a most convincing love of the thing he is doing.

PLATES

I. *New Amsterdam*, 1650 BY LAURENS BLOCK (?)

2. *Troop Maneuvers* BY JOHN SINGLETON COPLEY

3. *Mrs. Ebenezer Storer* BY JOHN SINGLETON COPLEY

4. *Cosimo III de Medici* BY JOHN SMIBERT

5. *Head of the Earl of Bathurst* BY JOHN SINGLETON COPLEY

6. *Central Figure for Monmouth before James II* BY JOHN SINGLETON COPLEY

7. *Brooke Watson and the Shark* BY JOHN SINGLETON COPLEY

8. *The Death of Major Pierson* BY JOHN SINGLETON COPLEY

9. *Head of an Old Man* BY BENJAMIN WEST

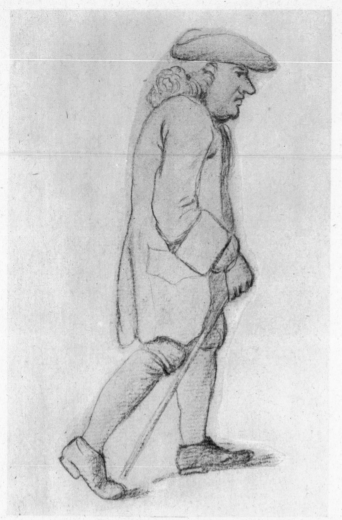

10. *David James Dove* BY BENJAMIN WEST

11. *Doctor Bragg* BY BENJAMIN WEST

12. *Figure Composition* BY BENJAMIN WEST

13. *The Three Sisters* BY BENJAMIN WEST

14. *Self Portrait* BY GILBERT STUART

Ferry 3 miles below Bristol.
drawn 1777: by CW.

15. *Ferry Three Miles below Bristol* BY CHARLES WILLSON PEALE

16. *Death of Hotspur* BY JOHN TRUMBULL

17. *Reclining Nude* BY JOHN TRUMBULL

18. *General Hugh Mercer* BY JOHN TRUMBULL

19. *Officers Crying* BY JOHN TRUMBULL

20. *Harpers Ferry in 1812* BY REMBRANDT PEALE

21. *Mrs. Richard C. Morse and Two Children, Elizabeth and Charlotte* BY SAMUEL F. B. MORSE

22. *Francis Grice* BY JOHN NEAGLE

23. *Self Portrait* BY EDWARD G. MALBONE

24. *Sarah Russell Church* BY JOHN VANDERLYN

25. *Romantic Landscape* BY WASHINGTON ALLSTON

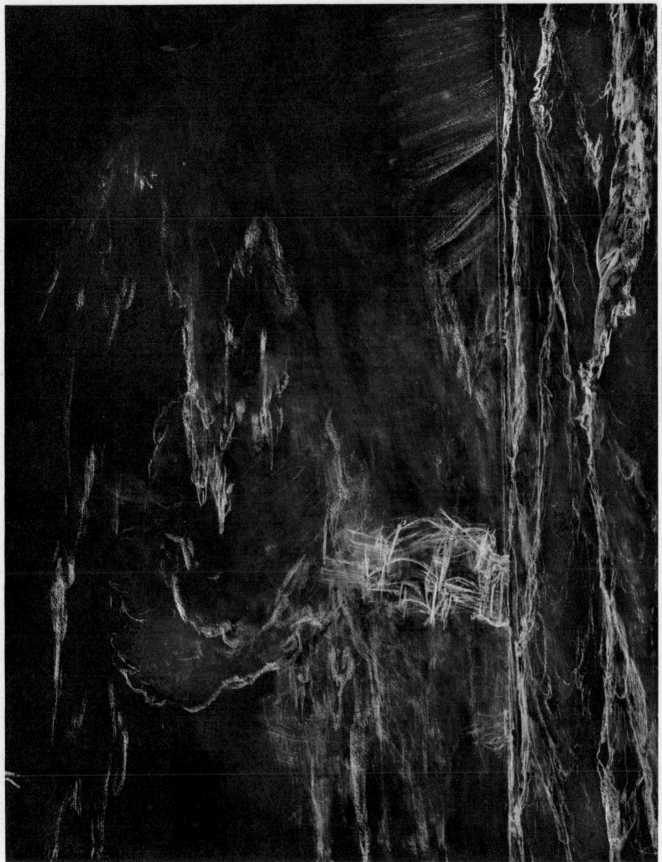

26. *Ships at Sea* BY WASHINGTON ALLSTON

27. *Broadway and Trinity Church, 1830* by John W. Hill.

28. *Sketch Sheet* BY THOMAS SULLY

29. *Portrait of a Man* BY HENRY INMAN

30. *Woman and Child Reading* BY THOMAS SULLY

Robert Owen — a Study from Life — London 1833.

31. *Portrait Sketch of Robert Owen* BY REMBRANDT PEALE

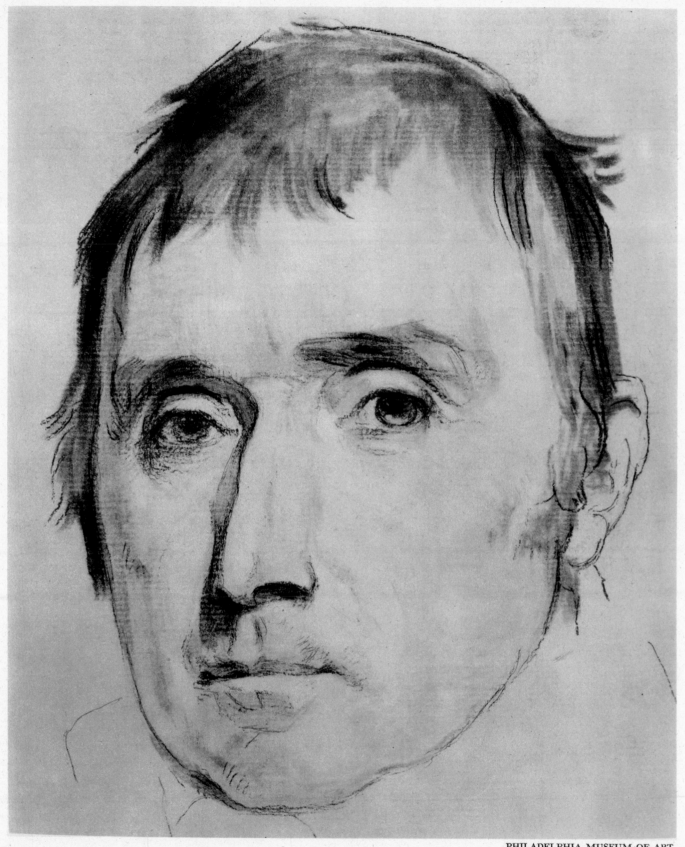

32. *Man's Head* BY THOMAS SULLY

33. *River Scene* BY THOMAS DOUGHTY

34. *Romantic Scene* BY SAMUEL F. B. MORSE

35. *Illustration for The Betrothed* BY HENRY INMAN

36. *Sketches* BY JOHN NEAGLE

Red Jacket, taken from life in the Spring of 1823.
Presented to R.V. DeWitt by his friend Henry Inman.

37. *Red Jacket* BY HENRY INMAN

38. *An Indian Girl of the 'Iowas of the Missouri'* BY C. B. J. DE ST. MEMIN

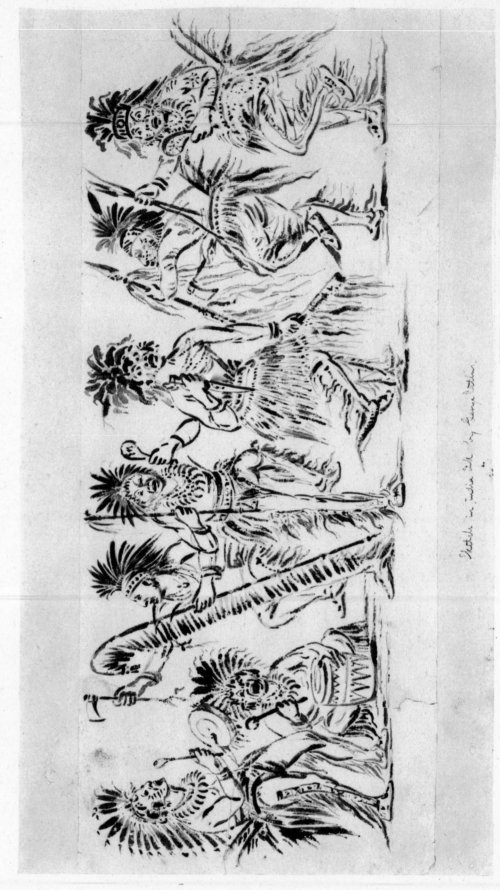

39. *War Dance* BY GEORGE CATLIN

40. *Landscape* BY ASHER B. DURAND

41. *The Heart of the Andes* BY FREDERICK E. CHURCH

42. *Landscape* BY THOMAS COLE

43. *Seascape*
BY FREDERICK E. CHURCH

44. *Rural Scene* BY ASHER B. DURAND

45. *Sketch from Nature* BY ASHER B. DURAND

Thomas Cole.

46. *Landscape with Tower* BY THOMAS COLE

78

47. *Ivory-Billed Woodpecker* BY JOHN JAMES AUDUBON

48. *Horse* BY ANONYMOUS ARTIST

49. *Sketch for The Stump Speaker* BY GEORGE CALEB BINGHAM

50. *Sketch for The Stump Speaker* BY GEORGE CALEB BINGHAM

51. *Ginger Beer Stall* BY DAVID CLAYPOOLE JOHNSTON

52. *Conestoga Wagon* BY FELIX O. C. DARLEY

54. *Sketch for Raftsmen Playing Cards by George Caleb Bingham*

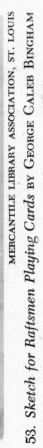

53. *Sketch for Raftsmen Playing Cards by George Caleb Bingham*

55. *Portrait of a Lady* BY WILLIAM SIDNEY MOUNT

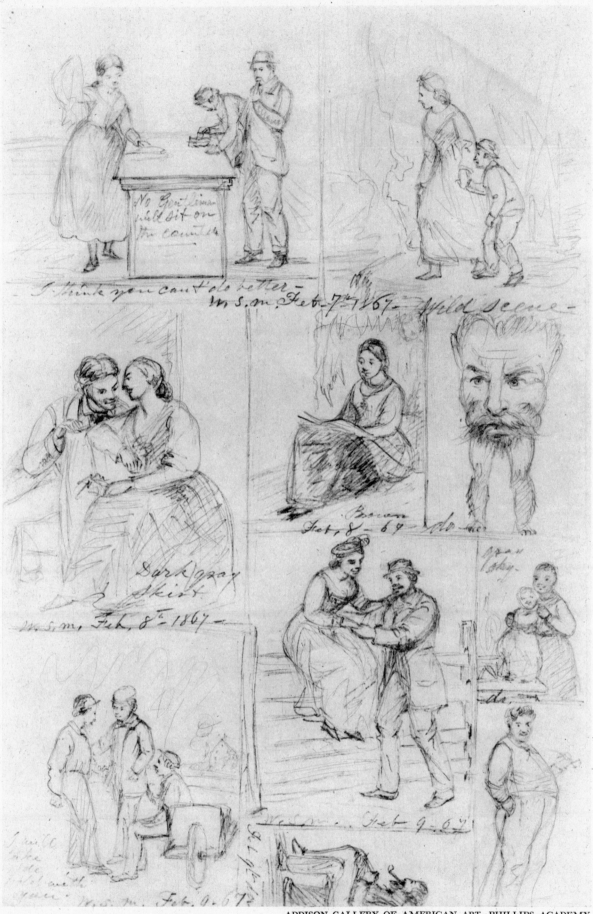

56. *Sketches* BY WILLIAM SIDNEY MOUNT

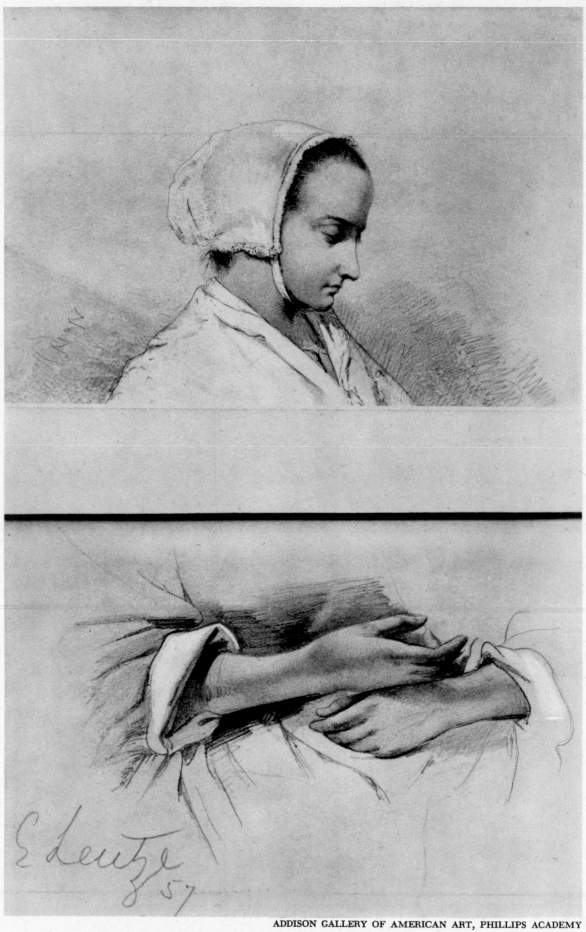

57. *Head of a Woman* BY EMANUEL LEUTZE

58. *Midshipman Seabury* BY WILLIAM SIDNEY MOUNT

59. *Sketch for The Bathers* BY WILLIAM MORRIS HUNT

60. *Portrait Study* BY WILLIAM MORRIS HUNT

61. *Polly Gary* BY EASTMAN JOHNSON

62. *The Unruly Calf* BY WINSLOW HOMER

63. *Berry Pickers* BY EASTMAN JOHNSON

64. *Secretary Dobbins* BY EASTMAN JOHNSON

65. *Miss Ward* BY EASTMAN JOHNSON

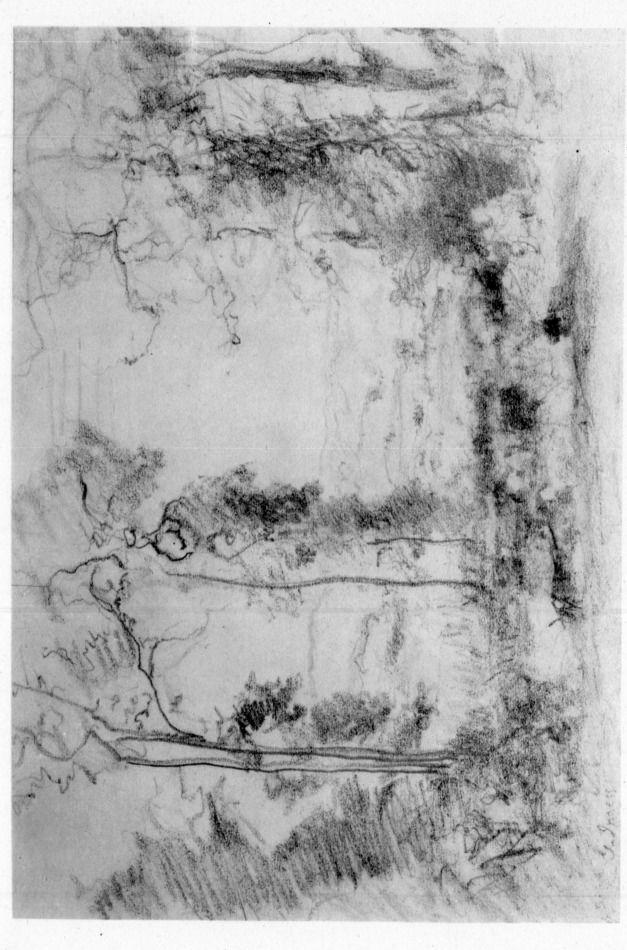

66. *Woodland Bank* BY GEORGE INNESS

67. *Landscape* BY GEORGE INNESS

68. *Nude with a Fan* BY J. A. McNeill Whistler

Croquis du Portrait de Carlyle .

69. *Sketch for the Portrait of Carlyle* BY J. A. McNEILL WHISTLER

70. *Venetian Canal* BY J. A. McNEILL WHISTLER

71. *Street Scene* by Homer Martin

72. *Figure Studies* BY JOHN LA FARGE

73. *The Three Marys* by JOHN LA FARGE

74. *Sketch in the Adirondacks* BY HOMER MARTIN

75. *The Last Boat In* by WINSLOW HOMER

76. *Study of a Soldier* BY WINSLOW HOMER

77. *Boy Picking Berries* BY WINSLOW HOMER

78. *Banks Fishermen* BY WINSLOW HOMER

79. *Flamboro Head, England* BY WINSLOW HOMER

Drawing in India Ink
by Thomas Eakins
1876

80. *Study for The Gross Clinic* BY THOMAS EAKINS

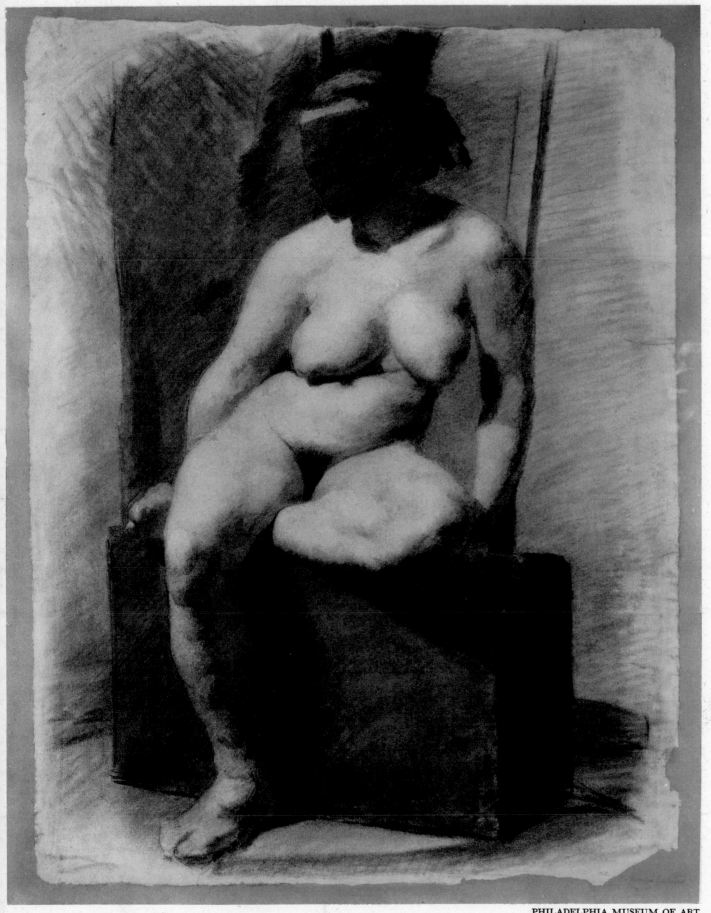

81. *Masked Woman Seated* BY THOMAS EAKINS

82. *Spanish Peak, Colorado* BY THOMAS MORAN

83. *Wind-Blown Pines, Pacific Grove, California* BY SAMUEL COLMAN

84. *Tammany Tiger* BY THOMAS NAST

85. *Two Deer Lying Down* BY RALPH ALBERT BLAKELOCK

86. *Study for The Boy Lincoln* BY EASTMAN JOHNSON

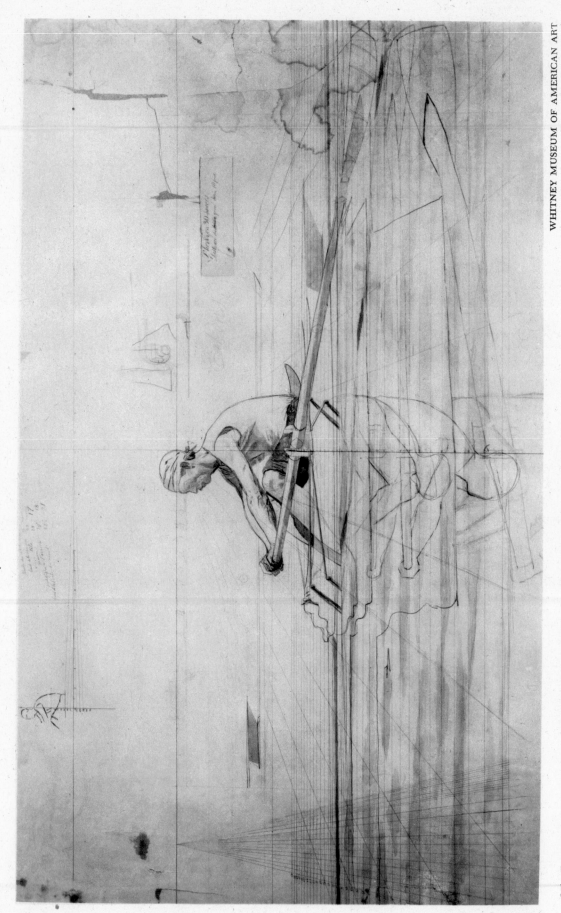

87. *Perspective Drawing and Study of John Biglen* BY THOMAS EAKINS

88. *Negro Boy Dancing* BY THOMAS EAKINS

89. *Double Self Portrait by* FRANK DUVENECK

90. *Head of a Girl* BY THOMAS WILMER DEWING

91. *Head of a Young Girl* BY FRANK DUVENECK

92. *Seated Woman* BY WILLIAM M. CHASE

93. *Girl at the Piano* BY J. ALDEN WEIR

94. *Girl Seated* BY MARY CASSATT

95. *Little Church around the Corner* BY CHILDE HASSAM

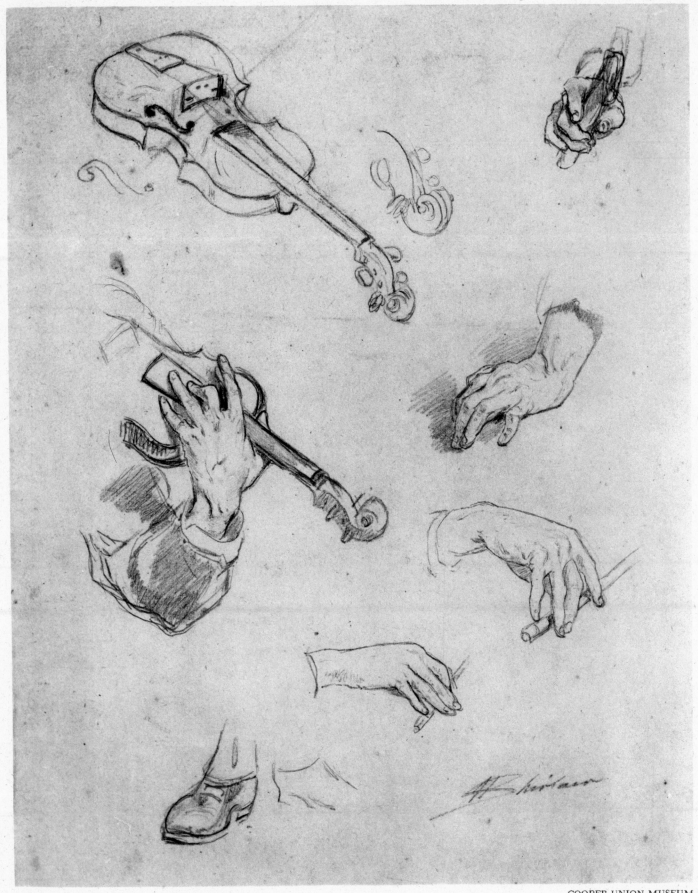

96. *Studies for Violin Player* BY WALTER SHIRLAW

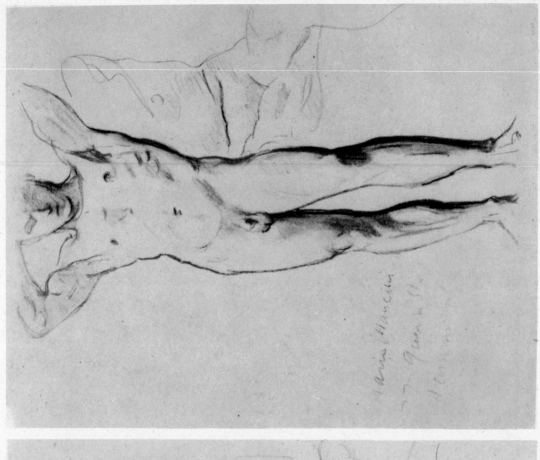

98. *Figure Study: Man Standing, Hands on Head* BY JOHN SINGER SARGENT

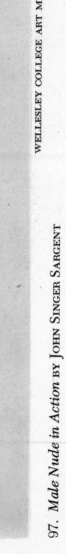

97. *Male Nude in Action* BY JOHN SINGER SARGENT

99. *Duchess of Marlborough* BY JOHN SINGER SARGENT

100. *Madison Square*, 1892 BY CHARLES JAY TAYLOR

101. *Footbridge at Bridgeport* BY JOHN H. TWACHTMAN

102. *A New England Regiment Taking the Cars from Jersey City for the Front, April, 1864* BY EDWARD LAMSON HENRY

103. *On the Shore* BY MAURICE PRENDERGAST

104. *Street Bathers* BY GLENN O. COLEMAN

105. *Studies of Men's Heads* BY GEORGE LUKS

106. *Washington Square*, 1914 BY WILLIAM J. GLACKENS

108. *The Apple Seller* BY WILLIAM J. GLACKENS

107. *The Boatman* BY ROBERT HENRI

109. *L. Waterbury at Polo* BY GEORGE LUKS

110. *McSorley's Cats* BY JOHN SLOAN

111. *State Police in Philadelphia* BY JOHN SLOAN

ADDISON GALLERY OF AMERICAN ART, PHILLIPS ACADEMY

112. *The Shovellers* BY MAHONRI YOUNG

WHITNEY MUSEUM OF AMERICAN ART

113. *Conversation* BY GUY PENE DU BOIS

114. *Dempsey through the Ropes* BY GEORGE BELLOWS

115. *Old Chinatown Restaurant* BY EVERETT SHINN

116. *The Jury* BY GEORGE OVERBURY ('POP') HART

117. *Adrift* BY EUGENE HIGGINS

118. *Study for Manhattan Bridge Loop* BY EDWARD HOPPER

120. *Head* BY JOHN CARROLL

119. *Woman Clown* BY WALT KUHN

121. *Jean* BY GEORGE BELLOWS

122. *Landscape: Mount Katahdin* BY MARSDEN HARTLEY

123. *Eagle Claw and Bean Necklace* BY GEORGIA O'KEEFFE

124. *Head of a Woman* BY MAX WEBER

125. *The Master of the House* BY BOARDMAN ROBINSON

126. *Frontier Guard, Macedonia* BY BOARDMAN ROBINSON

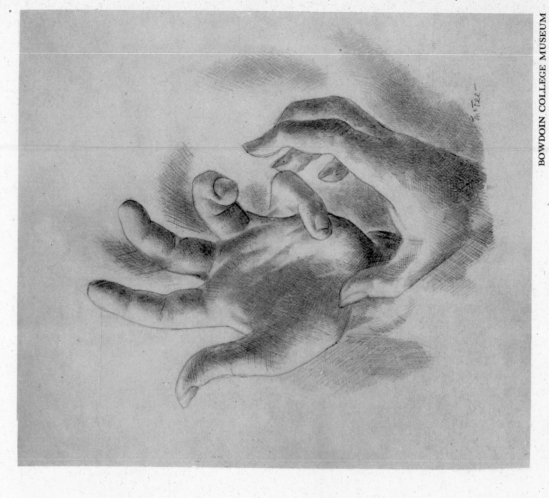

128. *Hands* BY HENRY LEE MCFEE

127. *The City* BY HENRY LEE MCFEE

130. *Balinese Girl* BY MAURICE STERNE

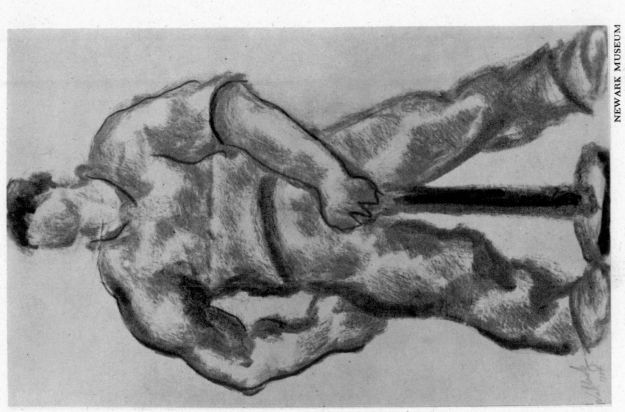

129. *Man of Iron* BY ABRAHAM WALKOWITZ

131. *It Was the Wrong Time to Say the Right Thing* BY BOARDMAN ROBINSON

132. *Self Portrait* BY PRESTON DICKINSON

134. *Study of a Head* BY MORRIS KANTOR

133. *Flower Study—Compote* BY STUART DAVIS

135. *Girl Walking* BY REGINALD MARSH

R Soyer

136. *Study of an Old Man* BY RAPHAEL SOYER

137. *Make-up* by ISABEL BISHOP

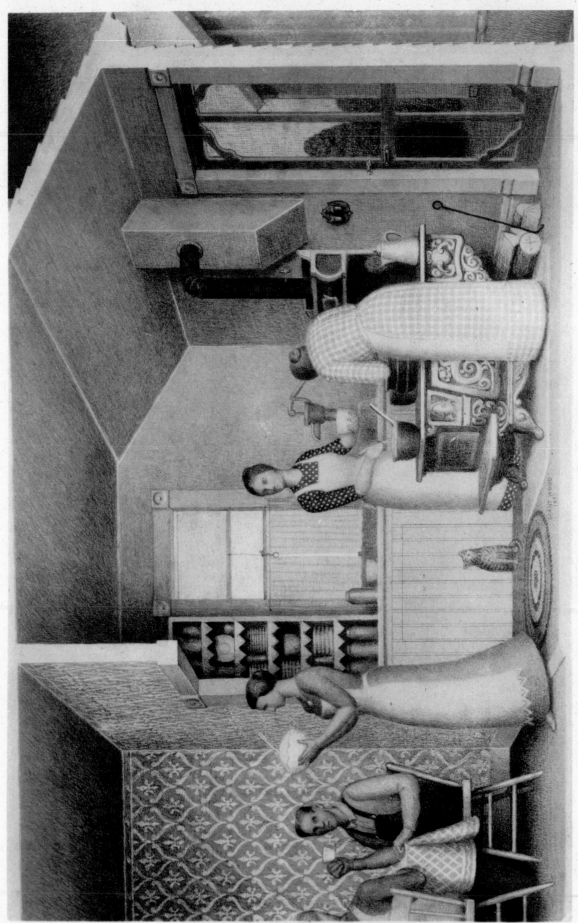

138. *Dinner for Threshers* BY GRANT WOOD

139. *Mississippi River #1* BY THOMAS BENTON

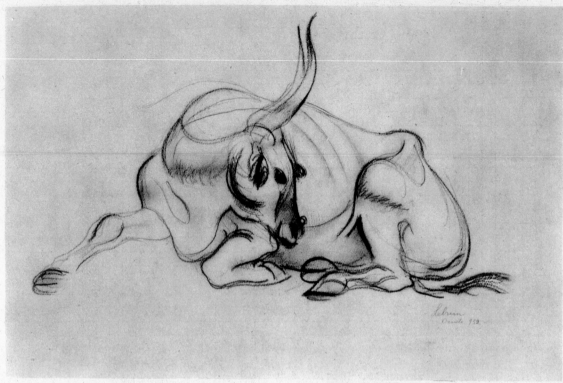

140. *Reclining Ox* BY RICO LEBRUN

141. *Whippet* BY JOHN B. FLANNAGAN

142. *Head of a Negro* BY JOHN STEUART CURRY

143. *Red Moore* BY EUGENE SPEICHER

144. *Conflict* by Jon Corbino

145. *Portrait Study* BY GEORGE GROSZ

146. *Blessed Damozel* BY PEGGY BACON

147. *Self Portrait* BY JULES PASCIN

148. *Lion Tamer* BY ALEXANDER CALDER

149. *Sunday Stroll* BY ADOLF DEHN

150. *Skaters* BY YASUO KUNIYOSHI

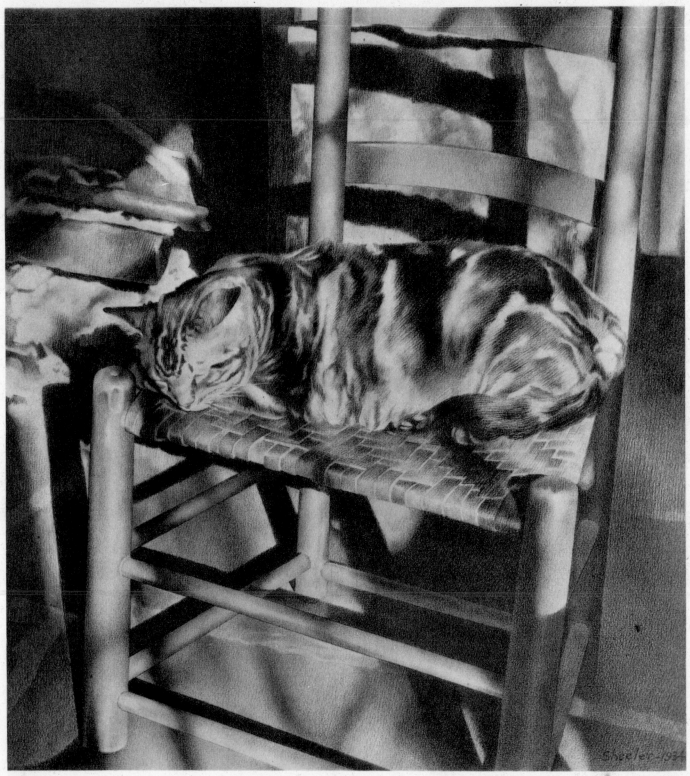

151. *Feline Felicity* BY CHARLES SHEELER

152. *Acrobats* BY CHAIM GROSS

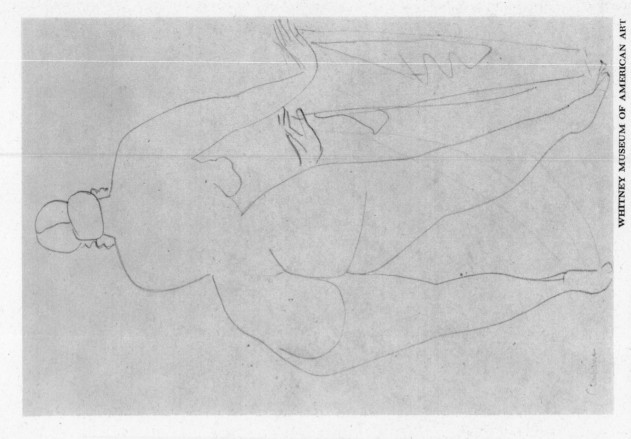

154. *Nude Study* BY GASTON LACHAISE

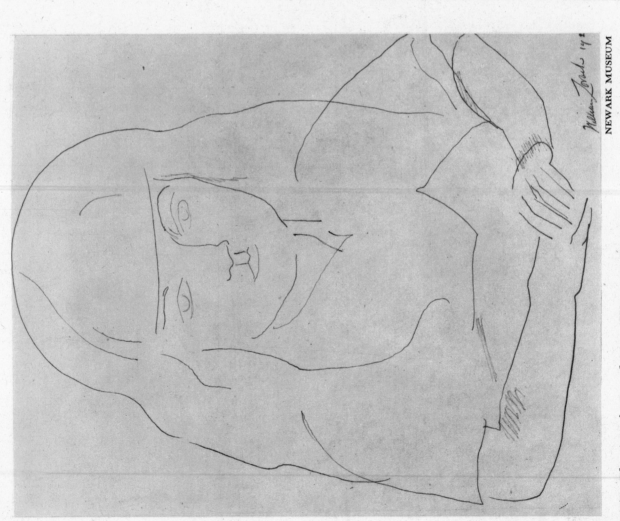

153. *The Artist's Daughter* BY WILLIAM ZORACH

155. *Engineers at Gaeta* BY MITCHELL SIPORIN

156. *Draped Nude* BY BOARDMAN ROBINSON

157. *Laughing Angel* BY JON CORBINO

158. *Rehab's Barns* BY PETER BLUME

159. *Lake and Trees* BY ADOLF DEHN

160. *Boxer* BY MAHONRI YOUNG

161. *Farmers' Revolt* BY WILLIAM GROPPER

162. *Air Raid* BY JOHN GROTH

163. *To the Lynching!* BY PAUL CADMUS